GIRLS' HOME SPA LAB

All-Natural Recipes, Healthy Habits, and Feel-Good Activities to Make You Glow

Maya Pagán

Storey Publishing

The mission of Storey Publishing is to serve our customers by
publishing practical information that encourages
personal independence in harmony with the environment.

EDITED BY Deanna F. Cook and Michal Lumsden
ART DIRECTION AND BOOK DESIGN BY Michaela Jebb
TEXT PRODUCTION BY Erin Dawson
INDEXED BY Christine R. Lindemer, Boston Road Communications

COVER PHOTOGRAPHY BY © Winky Lewis, except rose bath balls by Mars Vilaubi

INTERIOR PHOTOGRAPHY BY © Winky Lewis, except 16 right, 66, 67, 79 step 3, 82, 87 bottle, 88
label, 91 except top, 96, 99 bottom, 100, 101 bottle, 103, 105, 109, 115 razors, 121, 127, 136, 137 top, 140, 141
bottom, 144, 152, 155 by Mars Vilaubi

ADDITIONAL PHOTOGRAPHY BY © abzee/iStock.com, 64; © AlasdairJames/iStock.com, 101 salt;
© amirage/iStock.com, 68 right; © blackred/iStock.com, 74 bottom left; © CHAIWATPHOTOS/iStock
.com, 16 left; © dilananikolova/iStock.com, 27; © Floortje/iStock.com, 126 left; © gibgalich/iStock.com,
80 cucumbers; © janniwet/iStock.com, 26; © joakimbkk/iStock.com, 77 bottom; © JohnGollop/iStock.com,
68 center; © MidoSemsem/iStock.com, 87 honey; © popovaphoto/iStock.com, 151 pot; © shawn_hem-
pel/iStock.com, 65; © Ukususha/iStock.com, 37 right; © vikif/iStock.com, 151 bowl; © Vitalina/iStock.com,
134 lemons; © yorkfoto/iStock.com, 22 bottom, 129 top

PHOTO STYLING BY Catrine Kelty

ILLUSTRATIONS BY © Julz Nally, except © bsd555/iStock.com, 103, © Natalyon, backgrounds
throughout, and © saw/iStock.com, 120

© 2018 by Maya Pagán

Storey Publishing
210 MASS MoCA Way
North Adams, MA 01247
storey.com

Printed in China through Asia Pacific Offset
10 9 8 7 6 5 4 3 2 1

Library of Congress Cataloging-in-Publication Data

Names: Pagán, Maya, author.
Title: Girls' home spa lab : all-natural recipes, healthy
habits, and feel-good activities to make you glow /
Maya Pagán.
Description: North Adams, MA : Storey Publishing, [2018]
| Audience: Ages 9-13. | Includes index.
Identifiers: LCCN 2018021753 (print) | LCCN 2018032256
(ebook) | ISBN 9781635860894 (ebook) |
ISBN 9781612129648 (pbk. : alk. paper)
Subjects: LCSH: Beauty, Personal—Juvenile literature. |
Grooming for Girls—Juvenile literature. | Teenage
girls—Health and hygiene—Juvenile literature.
Classification: LCC RA777.25 (ebook) | LCC RA777.25 .P34
2018 (print) | DDC 613/.04243—dc23
LC record available at https://lccn.loc.gov/2018021753

This book is dedicated to my daughter, Noemi, who inspires me daily to make healthy choices and live life well.

CONTENTS

EVERYDAY WELLNESS 35

WAKE, PLAY, SLEEP 11

SELF CARE

SHINE BRIGHT

ABOUT FACE 55

HAIR CARE 83

YOU ARE BEAUTIFUL

HEALTHY HANDS & FEET 131

BODY-CARE CONCOCTIONS 107

APPENDIX

DISCOVER YOUR OWN BEAUTY

This book will help you discover your own beauty, from the inside out, with natural skin-care recipes and creative self-care projects to help you glow with health and happiness. Taking time to nurture your mind, body, and spirit is key to your overall well-being. Ultimately, self-care leads to wellness, and wellness leads to beauty. Making healthy choices about what you put *in* and *on* your body translates into a clear message that you matter — that YOU are important!

Everyone wants to feel healthy and beautiful, but the pressure to look like the glamorous pop-culture images can be frustrating and confusing. The beauty industry wants you to believe that it has all the answers, and it's willing to sell you quick "fixes" to real or imagined "problems." The truth is, there's no need to spend lots of money on fancy store-bought products or to schedule regular appointments at a spa to feel good and look good. You can take your health into your own hands!

I learned this when I was a young teenager. Walking home from school every day, I passed a drugstore. I'd often cruise the aisles searching for something to help with the pimples that were arriving with my changing skin. I never had enough money in my wallet to afford the creams, so I got resourceful. In a teen magazine I read an article about making facial masks out of common kitchen ingredients. I tried a few recipes and was hooked — right away! Making my own skin-care products was easy and almost free, and I knew exactly what I was putting on my face. Plus, my skin was clearer, smoother, and happier.

I've been making homemade masks and other skin-care products ever since. These days I'm creating them with my teenage daughter and all of her friends, and we'd like to teach you how, too. When you make something by hand, you feel a deeper connection to it and appreciation for it when you use it. DIY is totally empowering, not to mention fun! Invite a couple of friends over and share a home spa afternoon with facials, homemade hair treatments, and soothing pedicures.

My recipes and instructions are easy to follow and often call for familiar ingredients that are good enough to eat — like honey, oats, coconut oil, sugar, and strawberries. Because the products you'll make are all natural, with no preservatives, you should use them up within a few weeks. Store them in a cool, dry place, and discard immediately if you notice they have changed colors or smell unpleasant.

Within these pages you'll find everything you need to become your own wellness expert. You'll learn to how to convert your kitchen into a laboratory for crafting customized cleansers, lotions, and hair products. You'll discover tips for sleeping better and relaxing more. You'll even be able to transform your bathroom into a sanctuary for winding down and recharging.

True wellness comes from radiant health and loving yourself — and the skin you're in. Are you ready to glow?

Maya Pagán

WAKE*
PLAY*SLEEP

Just as there are different seasons to the year, there are different rhythms to each day. Discovering how to flow through each day with balanced energy and then fall asleep with ease can transform how you feel about yourself and your life. This chapter is filled with routines and recipes to help you feel great from dawn to dusk.

Know Yourself

Good Mornings!

A fresh new day deserves a good beginning. Here are five ways to get off to the best start possible.

Avoid screen time in the early morning.

Set your alarm early enough to give yourself plenty of time to get ready for the day.

Stretch your body. Do yoga.

Eat a healthy breakfast.

Write down at least one positive thought in a morning journal.

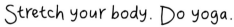

JOT IT DOWN
Morning Gratitude

Keep a notebook by the side of your bed, and take a few minutes each morning to write down several things you're thankful for. This could end up being the most valuable part of your day. It's been shown that taking the time to practice gratitude has huge benefits, including:

+ Greater happiness and reduced depression

+ Improved relationships and self-esteem

+ Sounder sleep

+ Better physical health

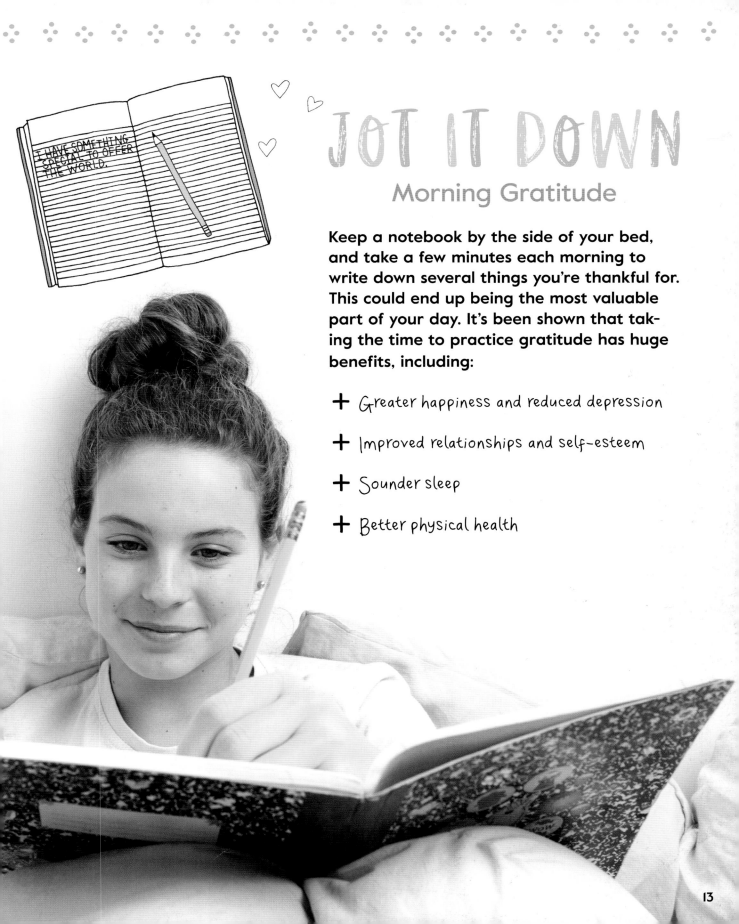

I HAVE SOMETHING SPECIAL TO OFFER THE WORLD.

MORNING YOGA

Moving around first thing in the morning helps both your body and your mind wake up. Try the following series of movements to start your day feeling refreshed.

Earthbound Sun Salutation

You can roll onto the floor or even stay right in bed to do this sequence of poses. Start each movement on an inhalation or an exhalation, following the rhythm of your own breath.

Learn the Poses

Kneeling prayer pose. Sit very still, let your body get quiet, and notice your breathing. Feel the weight of your "sit bones" (at the base of your pelvis) resting evenly on your heels.

Kneeling sky reach. Lift your arms as you rise up onto your knees. Reach for the sky, looking above you and keeping your spine long.

Puppy pose. Keeping your hips over your knees, drop your forehead to the floor, and reach your hands out in front of you. Feel the stretch from your palms to your hips.

Cat pose. Press your hands and knees down as you lift up your core (your abdomen), rounding your back and tucking in your tailbone and your head.

Do the Poses

1. Kneeling prayer pose.
2. Kneeling sky reach.
3. Puppy pose.
4. Cat pose.
5. Puppy pose.
6. Kneeling sky reach.
7. Kneeling prayer pose.

Repeat the whole sequence once more.

WAKE-UP FACIAL SPRITZER

MAKES ½ CUP

This spritzer may be more effective than caffeine! Give your face a refreshing spray (with your eyes closed) before you even sit down for breakfast, and you'll be ready for the day.

WHAT YOU NEED

3 tablespoons aloe vera gel

3 tablespoons witch hazel

3 drops peppermint essential oil

HOW YOU MAKE IT

Combine the aloe vera gel, witch hazel, and essential oil in a spritzer bottle and shake well. Store in the refrigerator. Shake before using.

SMOOTHIE BOWL

MAKES 2½ CUPS

Using a blender is the fast and easy way to a healthy morning. Extra-thick smoothies call for a bowl rather than a glass. You can also forget straws; use a spoon instead, and add fun toppings for a fresh twist on breakfast.

WHAT YOU NEED

1–2 frozen bananas

1 cup yogurt or milk

1 cup berries, fresh or frozen

1 handful fresh spinach (optional)

Toppings of your choice, such as chia seeds, granola, toasted almonds, coconut flakes or shavings, or fresh fruit

HOW YOU MAKE IT

1. Combine all of the ingredients except the toppings in a blender. Blend on high speed until the mixture is creamy and smooth.

2. Pour into a bowl and decorate with your toppings of choice. Enjoy!

TRY THIS

Some skin-care recipes call for a small amount of coconut milk. You can save the left-over coconut milk from those recipes to use in your morning smoothie bowl in place of the yogurt or milk.

Know Yourself

Sweet Dreams!

Busy schedules, too much homework, and friendship drama can make it hard to fall asleep. Stop tossing and turning after the lights go out by creating a routine around your favorite recipes and projects from this section. Repeating the routine each night will help train your body and mind to relax on schedule. Here's a five-step plan for catching your Zs with ease!

Stop looking at screens and devices at least 1 hour before you get into bed.

Drink a warm beverage before bedtime. Try one of the sleep potions on the following pages.

Slow your body down in the evening with simple yoga poses (page 28).

Soak in the bathtub before bedtime. Try the calming Tub Tea (page 120).

Use scents to increase your peace.
The Lavender Sleep Mask (page 23) and Sweet Dreams Spray (page 27) both use aroma to encourage a quiet mind and relaxed body once you're tucked into bed.

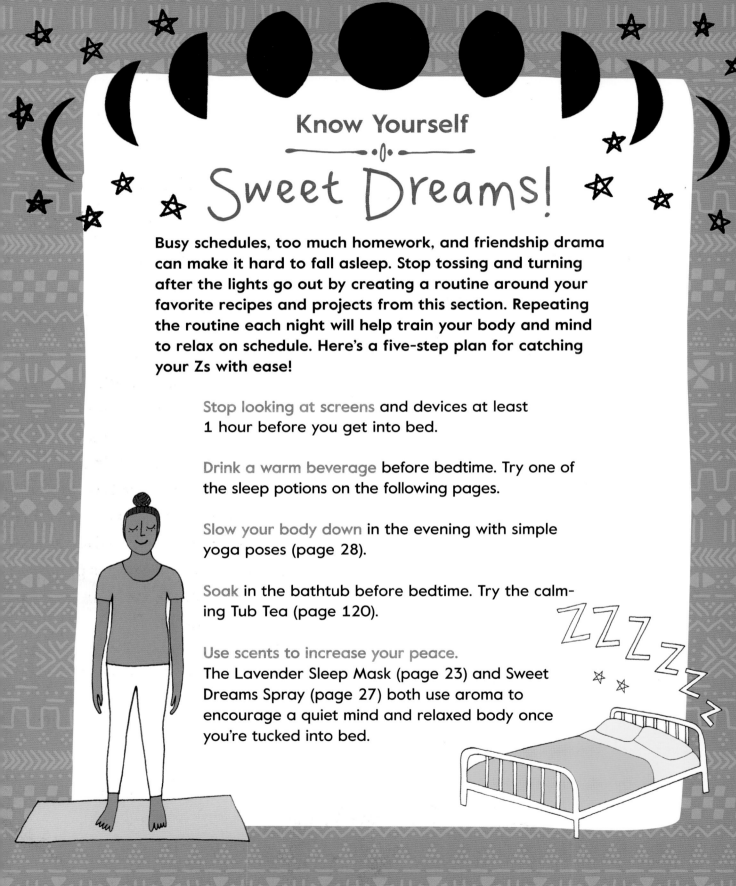

Sleep Potions

Getting a good night's sleep is essential for health and well-being. A warm beverage just before bedtime can help make that happen. These sleep-inducing recipes use relaxing, calming ingredients to help your body and mind wind down naturally.

SLEEP TIGHT TEA

MAKES ¼ CUP DRY HERB MIXTURE

This blend of herbs will surely send you off to dreamland. Drink this tea as is, or sweeten it lightly with a drop of honey. If you want to have the tea ready to enjoy regularly, triple the herb measurements and store the mixture in a glass jar with a tight lid. You can find all of these dried herbs in the bulk section of most natural food stores.

HOW YOU MAKE IT

1. Combine all the herbs in a glass jar, seal tightly, and shake to mix well. Any leftover herbs can be stored in the jar for future cups of tea.

2. Place 2 teaspoons of the herb mixture in a tea ball or tea basket, and set it in a mug.

3. Boil the water and pour over the herb mixture. Let steep for 5 minutes, then remove the herbs and drink the tea.

WHAT YOU NEED

1 **tablespoon dried chamomile**

1 **tablespoon dried lemon balm**

1 **tablespoon dried peppermint**

1 **teaspoon fennel seeds**

1 **teaspoon dried rose petals**

1½ **cups water**

BANANA DEEP SLEEP TEA

MAKES 2 CUPS

Bananas are filled with potassium and magnesium, which work together to relax muscles and calm the nervous system. The result? The right conditions for sweet dreams. This tea works so well because it uses the banana peel, where these powerhouse minerals are stored. Find a quiet place to relax while you sip your bedtime brew.

WHAT YOU NEED

- 1 ripe banana (preferably organic, since you'll use the peel)
- 2 cups water

  Sprinkle of ground cinnamon

HOW YOU MAKE IT

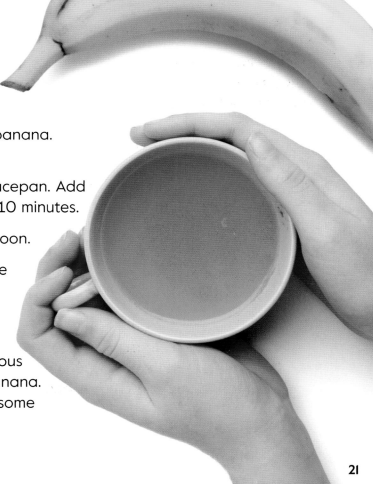

1. Cut off and discard both ends of the banana. Leave the peel on.

2. Bring the water to a boil in a small saucepan. Add the banana to the water and boil for 10 minutes.

3. Remove the banana using a slotted spoon.

4. Pour the hot water into a mug. Add the cinnamon, stir, and enjoy!

TRY THIS

For added relaxation benefits and a delicious nighttime snack, you can eat the boiled banana. Peel it open, discard the skin, and sprinkle some additional cinnamon on the fruit.

GOLDEN MILK

MAKES 2 CUPS

This warm drink will help you unwind at the end of the day and get a good night's sleep. Turmeric aids digestion, boosts your immune system, balances your mood, and eases aches and pains. Serve this in a mug and have a restful night!

WHAT YOU NEED

2 cups milk (coconut, almond, or dairy)

1 teaspoon raw honey or maple syrup

1 teaspoon ground turmeric

½ teaspoon ground cinnamon

¼ teaspoon powdered ginger or ½ teaspoon grated fresh ginger

Pinch of black pepper

Pinch of cayenne pepper

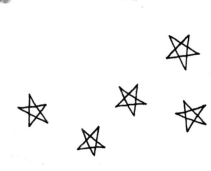

HOW YOU MAKE IT

1. Combine the milk, honey, turmeric, cinnamon, ginger, black pepper, and cayenne pepper in a blender and mix until frothy, about 1 minute on high speed.

2. Pour the mixture into a saucepan. Heat it up slowly, being careful not to let it boil. Drink warm.

Lavender Sleep Mask

This gentle sleep aid gives the scents and sense of falling asleep in a field of blooming lavender. It also blocks out light so you can sleep in on the weekend or take a good catnap.

WHAT YOU NEED

+ Pattern for Sleep Mask (see inside back cover)

+ 8- by 10-inch piece of fleece

+ Colored marker

+ Scissors

+ 15-inch length of elastic

+ Straight pins

+ Thread

+ Sewing needle

+ 3–5 tablespoons dried lavender

HOW YOU MAKE IT

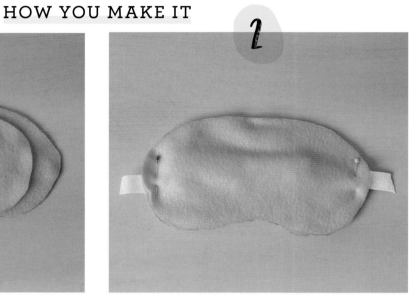

Trace the pattern twice onto your fabric, using a marker, and then cut out both pieces. Place the fabric pieces together with what will be the outside faces on the inside, turned toward each other.

Sandwich the elastic between the two fabric pieces, leaving a short length sticking out from each side. Pin the fabric pieces and elastic in place.

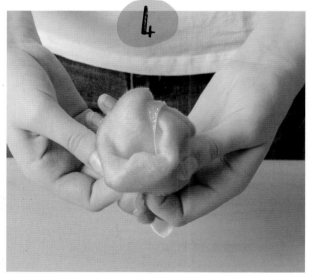

Thread a needle and stitch around the fabric about ¼ inch in from the edge. Stop stitching about 2 inches before you complete the circumference of the mask.

Reach a finger or two through the opening and pull the mask right-side out. The strip of elastic should now be on the outside of the mask.

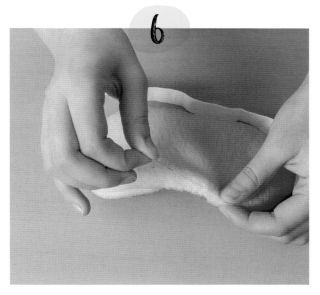

Shape the mask by poking out the edges that are tucked in at the seam, then fill it with the lavender.

At the opening that remains, tuck the edges of fabric inward. Sew the opening closed with tiny stitches.

SLEEP WELL!

Peaceful Pillow

When the lights go out, your pillowcase will light up with a glowing bedtime message.

WHAT YOU NEED

+ 1 pillowcase
+ Pencil
+ Paper
+ Glow-in-the-dark fabric pen or paint

HOW YOU MAKE IT

1. Decide what message you want on your pillowcase. Practice your design with a pencil and paper to get an idea of size and placement.

2. When you feel satisfied with your paper testing, write or paint directly on the pillowcase. Follow the instructions on the pen or paint packaging for heat setting and washing.

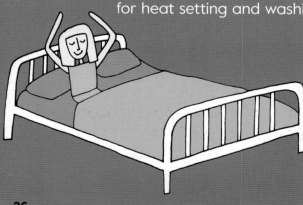

Sweet Dreams

Relax

DREAM BIG

Sleep Tight

Good Night

FOLLOW YOUR DREAMS

Twinkle, Twinkle

SWEET DREAMS SPRAY

MAKES ½ CUP

Spritz this blend on your pillow or around your room before bedtime to reduce stress, calm your nerves, and relax deeply.

WHAT YOU NEED

¼ cup distilled or purified water

2 tablespoons witch hazel

6 drops lavender essential oil

4 drops Roman chamomile essential oil

4 drops sweet orange essential oil

HOW YOU MAKE IT

Combine all the ingredients in a small spray bottle and shake. Shake before using.

STRESS BOARD

Keep a small chalkboard near your bed to use on those nights when you're really struggling to wind down.

Write on the chalkboard what's bugging you or what you're worrying about, and tell yourself that you'll deal with it in the morning.

The act of writing it down may free you from holding on to the worry. Knowing you'll get to it in the morning helps you let go. If it's still bothersome when the sun comes up, you will have had a night to sleep on it. If you feel like you're ready to move on, simply erase it from your board!

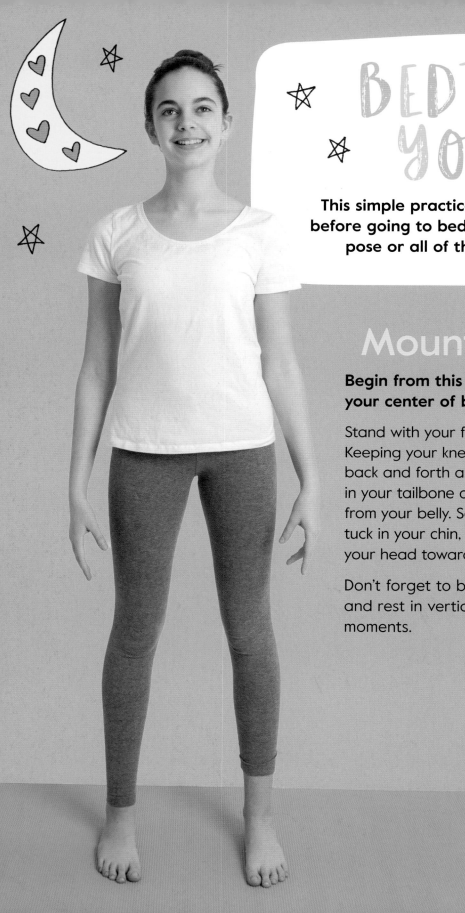

BEDTIME YOGA

This simple practice will help you relax before going to bed. You can do just one pose or all of them in sequence.

Mountain Pose

Begin from this basic position to find your center of balance.

Stand with your feet hip-width apart. Keeping your knees unlocked, gently rock back and forth and from side to side. Tuck in your tailbone and lift your chest away from your belly. Soften your shoulders, tuck in your chin, and reach the crown of your head toward the ceiling.

Don't forget to breathe. Close your eyes and rest in vertical stillness for a few moments.

Forward Fold

Next, practice this pose of deep release to get rid of tension and build your relaxation.

Standing with your feet hip-width apart, inhale and raise your hands above your head. Exhale and hinge forward at your hips, keeping your knees softly bent. Reach the crown of your head toward the floor, letting your arms dangle.

Breathe slowly. Imagine the top of your head opening and letting out all the busy thoughts from your mind. Grasp both elbows and softly rock side to side.

Child's Pose

Sink into this restful pose to restore balance and harmony to your body and your mind. Remain in it for as long as it feels comfortable.

Kneel on the floor with your bottom resting on your heels. Exhale and lean forward until your forehead reaches the ground. Let your arms rest at your sides. Loosen and soften everywhere.

Bring your awareness to your breath. With every exhalation, feel your forehead gently meeting the floor. Relax and let go.

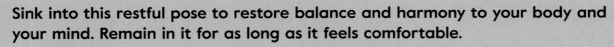

Legs Up the Wall

This pose redirects blood circulation to the upper body and head, which is especially helpful after a busy day. Do this right before you go to sleep, perhaps even from your bed!

Have a folded blanket handy and find an open wall. Slowly lie down on your back and extend your legs so that your feet face up and the backs of your legs are against the wall. If you need extra support under your back, lift up your hips and slide in the folded blanket.

Let your body soften. Rest your arms at your sides and let the back of your head be heavy.

Close your eyes. Breathe deeply through your nose. Stay here for 5 to 10 minutes.

To come out of this pose, push your body a few inches away from the wall and let your knees fall to your chest. Gently roll to one side with your knees still folded. Slowly return to sitting.

Dream Jar

Some nights, sleep just won't come, no matter how hard you try. Often your mind is racing with thoughts from the day or worries about tomorrow. When you've tossed and turned one too many times, bring out this Dream Jar and grab some inspiration for focusing your mind. Randomly select a slip of paper, and let the message guide you toward your dreams.

WHAT YOU NEED

+ 15 small sheets of pretty paper

+ Pen

+ Glass jar (or a container of any kind)

HOW YOU MAKE IT

1. On each piece of paper, write down one of your favorite things to think about.

2. Fold up the pieces of paper and tuck them into the jar.

3. Decorate the jar however you want.

WISH UPON A JAR

Here are some examples of what you might include in your Dream Jar. Fill in the following sentences or come up with your own.

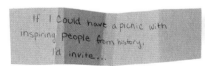
If I could have a picnic with inspiring people from history, I'd invite...

When I think of my favorite movie, I love remembering the scene where...

In 5 years I will be...

In 10 years I will be...

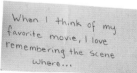
If I could go anywhere for summer vacation I'd go...

The last time I went to the beach I...

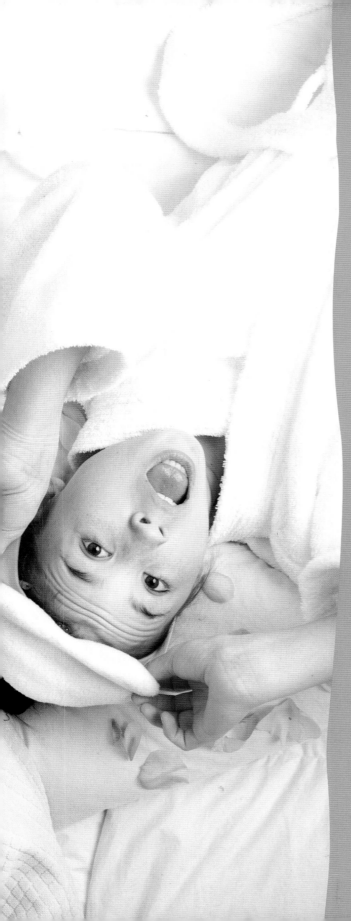

SPA SLEEPOVER ~ PARTY ~

Have some friends over for a night of pajamas and pampering. Here's what's on the agenda:

⚡ Make

Peaceful Pillows (page 26) — Have guests bring their own pillowcases.

Spa Slippers (page 145) — Have all the materials you'll need ready to go.

⚡ Do

Facials — Make and use cleansers, scrubs, steams, and masks from the About Face chapter (page 55).

Bedtime Yoga (page 28) — Put on some quiet music at the same time.

⚡ Drink

Sleep Potions (page 19) — Concoct a bedtime brew.

⚡ Eat

Smoothie Bowls (page 17) — Enjoy these treats for breakfast the next day.

EVERYDAY WELLNESS

Staying healthy and strong is easier when you take care of yourself from the inside out. This chapter is filled with useful ways to feel well all of the time. Whether you're facing an everyday illness or your monthly period, follow these tips and techniques to feel better fast!

Know Yourself

Healthy Habits to Live By

Each of these tips on its own can make a major contribution to your well-being. Put them all together and you'll feel amazing!

Stay hydrated.

Wash your hands frequently.

Eat whole, unprocessed foods.

Exercise.

Avoid sugar.

Get fresh air.

Sleep. A lot.

OH, BOTHER

QUICK FIXES FOR EVERYDAY ISSUES

There will always be things that annoy you. Having a toolbox filled with easy solutions will help you smooth out the rough spots in your day.

Feeling frazzled because you didn't understand last night's homework? Preoccupied with some friend drama?

Open up a bottle of lavender essential oil and gently inhale. And relax.

Need a nap, but don't have time to take one?

Open up a bottle of peppermint essential oil and gently inhale. And wake up.

Is something upsetting you or making you nervous, like an argument with someone you care about or a big test coming up?

Find a smooth stone or button and carry it in your pocket. When your mind starts running in circles, reach for it and rub it. Touching something solid helps ease your worries and focuses your thoughts.

BREATHE

RECHARGE

Starting your day off right will lessen the intensity of an afternoon slump, but as the day unfolds, you still might feel tired, stressed, or anxious. Here are 10 ways to keep your energy levels up and your mood mellow. Try to match a quiet activity with an energetic one for an unbeatable combination to help you get through the day happily.

+ **Drink up.** For a simple but fancy twist on regular old water, make some refreshing coolers. Just add chopped fruit (frozen is fine), slices of lemon, or chunks of cucumber to a pitcher or bottle of water and keep it chilling in the fridge.

+ **Eat a healthy, protein-rich snack.** Granola bars with nuts and fruit or just a handful of nuts can stop your stomach from growling and refuel your brain. Stay away from overly sweet snacks, as they'll wind you up and then make you crash.

+ **Breathe deeply.** Feed your body and your brain some extra oxygen to increase your energy levels and improve your mental performance. All you have to do is take 10 deep, slow breaths.

+ **Stretch.** Stand up. Roll your shoulders forward, then backward, while deeply breathing in and out. Repeat for 2 minutes. Next, inhale and reach your hands to the sky, then exhale and fold forward at your hips (page 29). Stay folded while you take several relaxed breaths. Slowly roll back up to standing.

+ **Unplug.** Ditch your phone for a while. In fact, take some time to leave all screens behind.

WATER ADD-IN IDEAS

 LEMON

 CUCUMBER

 MINT

 BERRIES

+ Organize something. Try straightening out your closet, your desk, or your bag. Pick something manageable and start sorting. Putting things in order will transform your energy.

+ Laugh! A good giggle or hardy chuckle can really give you a boost.

+ Have a private dance party. Put on your favorite music and shake it out.

+ Go outside. Walk out the door. Keep walking around the block or just around your yard for at least 10 minutes. Fresh air, sunlight, and movement will invigorate you and help reduce stress.

+ Meditate. Quieting and clearing the mind can help you find a sense of calm within and gain a better understanding of how you think about things. It also rejuvenates you when you are feeling worn out. See page 40 for a good meditation routine.

MINDFUL MOMENTS

Meditating doesn't have to be complicated. Begin with a short practice of a couple of minutes. Here are five easy steps to get you started.

1. **Pick a spot.** Choose somewhere quiet and private, like your bedroom or a special place in your backyard. Remove any clutter and distractions from the area.

2. **Sit comfortably.** There's no "correct" way to sit when you meditate. You can sit on the floor with your legs crossed. Or sit on your bed. Or in a chair. The most important thing is that you're comfortable and sitting upright.

3. **Clear your mind.** Close your eyes. Take a few deep breaths. Commit to spending some time letting go of the busy voice in your head and breathing deeply.

4. **Observe.** As you breathe, be aware of the thoughts that play through your mind. Let them float by and zigzag around, but don't engage with them. Simply watch them from a distance.

   When a thought catches your attention and you can't let it drift by, try simply counting each breath: 1 breath, 2 breaths, 3 breaths . . . When a thought peeks through and disturbs your counting, begin again from 1.

5. **Return to your day.** Take a few minutes to come back to your physical body and out of your head. Open your eyes softly. Roll your shoulders backward and then forward. Move your head from side to side and up and down. Allow this transition back to everyday life to be leisurely and gentle.

GET HEALTHY. GET HAPPY.

Squishy Stress Ball

Anxiety and worries can make you fidget. Having something to hold on to can help you focus and release that nervous energy. Keep one of these stress relievers in your pocket or at your homework station to boost your concentration. This project is so easy that you may as well make two — one for you and one for a friend!

WHAT YOU NEED

+ Funnel

+ 2 balloons per stress ball

+ 1 cup flour

+ Scissors

MAKE YOUR OWN FUNNEL

If you don't have a funnel but do have a used plastic water bottle, you can easily make your own funnel by cutting off the bottom of the water bottle and using the top.

HOW YOU MAKE IT

1

Secure the mouth of the funnel inside the neck of one balloon.

2

Pour the flour into the funnel until the balloon is full. Ease the neck of the balloon off the funnel. Gently squeeze out as much air as you can from the balloon without losing any flour.

3

Tie a knot in the balloon neck as close to the flour ball as possible.

4

Snip off the end of the balloon neck above the knot.

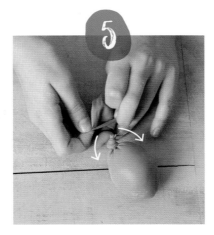

5

Cut off the neck of the second balloon, which will leave a small opening. Put the flour-filled balloon knot-side-first inside the empty balloon.

Done! Give it a satisfying squeeze!

43

Kick That Cold

A sore throat or a stuffy nose can be a sign that a cold is coming on. These two remedies can help you ward off illness, and they can also help you feel better when a cold takes you down.

HONEY LEMONADE THROAT SOOTHER

MAKES 3 CUPS

This healing combination of honey, lemon, and garlic can help soothe a sore, scratchy throat and ease a cough. Drink 1 cup while it's still hot, and drink the remaining 2 cups at room temperature throughout the day.

HOW YOU MAKE IT

1. Combine all the ingredients in a large pot with a lid. Set the pot over high heat, uncovered, until the water begins to boil.

2. Turn off the heat and cover the pot with the lid.

3. Let the mixture steep for 10 minutes before drinking.

WHAT YOU NEED

1 garlic clove, minced

2 tablespoons raw honey

1 whole lemon, sliced

3 cups water

Stuffy Nose Steam Pot

This easy steam will clear your sinuses when you have a cold or allergies. It can also warm you up when you feel chilled.

WHAT YOU NEED

+ 4–5 cups water

+ Tea kettle or large pot

+ 2 large towels

+ Large ceramic bowl

+ 2 peppermint tea bags or 2 tablespoons dried peppermint

+ ½ teaspoon fresh or dried rosemary

+ ½ teaspoon fresh or dried thyme

HOW YOU MAKE IT

1. Bring the water to a boil in a kettle or large pot.

2. In the meantime, set up a steaming station at your kitchen table. Fold one of the towels and place it on the table. Set the bowl on top of it. Place the tea bags and herbs in the bowl.

3. When the water is boiling, carefully pour it into the bowl.

HOW YOU USE IT

1. Sit down at the table and lean over the bowl. Drape the second towel over both your head and the bowl to trap the steam.

2. Steam for about 10 minutes. Keep your face close enough to the bowl so that you feel the steam, but not close enough to let the steam burn you. The steam should feel relaxing, not painful.

3. When you're ready, take off the towel, blow your nose, and splash cool water over your face.

ALL-NATURAL HEADACHE REMEDIES

Before reaching for any pills, try these steps to rid yourself of that pounding in your head.

+ Drink water. Lots of water.

+ Eat something quick and easy with protein, like a handful of nuts.

+ Reduce tension around your head by taking off glasses, hair ties, head bands, hats, or any other headgear.

+ Massage your temples, the bridge of your nose, and gently around your eyes.

+ Wrap yourself in a cozy blanket and put on your Lavender Sleep Mask (page 23). The scent of lavender is a great stress reliever.

MONTHLY EASE

Every girl experiences her period differently, but one thing we all share is enjoying a little extra comfort each month. Here are a few ideas for taking special care of yourself before and during your period to relieve the ache of cramps, lessen bloating, and guard against mood swings.

+ **Exercise regularly,** even during your period, to help relieve the anxiety, fatigue, and headaches that may come with your flow.

+ **Eat less salt,** especially before and during your period, so you don't feel bloated.

+ **Eat calcium-rich foods** such as green leafy veggies, yogurt, and sardines, all month long to help regulate your hormones.

+ **Drink raspberry leaf tea,** a simple remedy that women have used for centuries to ease cramps.

+ **Get plenty of sleep** during your period. You deserve it and your body needs it.

Monthly Salt & Petal Soak

Combine the healing properties of Epsom salt, which relieves muscle cramps and inflammation, with the beauty and scent of rose petals to transport you back to feeling 100 percent. If you can, find fresh organic roses from your garden or from a florist. Treat yourself to the luxury of bathing in fresh petals. Nothing feels more decadent!

WHAT YOU NEED

+ 1 cup Epsom salt

+ 1 handful rose petals, dried or fresh

WHAT YOU DO

Pour the Epsom salt into your bathtub and fill the tub with hot water. Toss in the rose petals. Get in and relax!

Hot Rice Pack

Use this long pillow when you need some relief from cramps. Heat it up in the microwave for about a minute, then drape it over your tummy or press it against your back.

WHAT YOU NEED

+ 1 worn pillowcase
+ Scissors
+ Sewing needle
+ Thread
+ 1–1½ pounds rice

HOW YOU MAKE IT

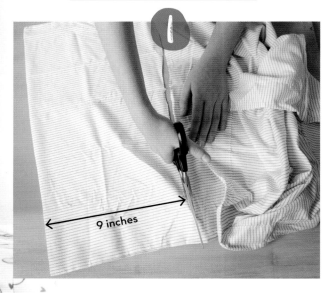

9 inches

Lay the pillowcase flat. Cut across the short side of the pillowcase, about 9 inches from the closed-up end (opposite the pillowcase opening).

Turn the pillowcase inside out and sew up the cut side with a simple running stitch. Leave a 6-inch opening in the center of your stitched seam.

Turn the pillowcase right side out, pulling through the opening.

Fill your pillowcase tube with rice. You want it to have some weight without being too heavy.

Close up the opening with tiny stitches.

TRY THIS

Here's a simple meditation you can do in 5 minutes:

- Sit quietly with your eyes closed.

- Become aware of your breath flowing in and out.

- See if you can lengthen each breath to a count of 4 for the in breath and another count of 4 for the out breath.

- Repeat this over and over again to feel the powerful shift of slowing, deepening, and being aware of your breathing rhythm.

STRESS BUSTERS

Stress weakens your immune system and can worsen PMS symptoms by increasing hormonal imbalances. Here are some basic de-stressors that you can try at any time of the month.

+ **Nature.** People who spend lots of time in nature have lower levels of cortisol, a stress hormone. Even many large cities have plenty of parks where you can walk. Go outside!

+ **Exercise.** Moving around is often an answer to what ails you, especially when it comes to stress. Exercise increases blood flow and raises levels of serotonin, a substance that is believed to contribute to feelings of happiness.

+ **Hobbies.** Do something you love. When you're enjoying yourself, your brain is satisfied, and there's less room for anxiety and stress.

+ **Breathing.** Giving your body lots of oxygen has a direct impact on your nervous system by feeding your cells with the nutrients they need for rebuilding. In addition, becoming conscious of your breathing — like when you're meditating — can help you feel more balanced.

ABOUT FACE

It's easier to feel confident when your skin is clear, smooth, and healthy. A pimple here and there happens to everyone, but the changing hormones and stress of adolescence increase the likelihood of big breakouts. This chapter is all about putting your best face forward. You'll learn how to create scrubs, cleansers, toners, and masks that match your skin's needs and keep it as healthy as possible.

Know Yourself

•◦•

Secrets to a Happy Face

Follow these steps to keep your face looking and feeling its best.

Keep it clean!

Cleanse your face at least twice a day, preferably when you wake up and before bedtime. The best time is right after you brush your teeth, so that you can wash away any stray toothpaste and oral bacteria.

After exercising, rinse away sweat with cool water.

Shower once a day to keep the oil from your hair and scalp from traveling to your face. To save time, keep an extra bottle of facial cleanser in the shower and wash your face while you're showering.

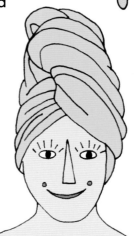

Hands off!

Get in the habit of not touching your face or resting your face on your hands. Your fingers and hands carry more germs than any other part of your body. When you touch your face, bacteria and dirt spread directly into your pores.

Avoid picking at bumps or pimples, no matter how tempting it is. You will only aggravate skin that is already irritated and inflamed.

Drink and eat wisely!

Eat whole foods, including lots of fresh vegetables and fruits. These nutrient-dense foods feed your skin the vitamins it needs to stay clear and healthy. Avoid greasy, sugary, and highly processed foods like pizza, French fries, potato chips, and candy.

Drink enough water to keep from being thirsty, especially when you exercise. Along with eating healthful foods and using a good moisturizer, drinking plenty of water will help ensure your skin stays clear, smooth, and dewy.

What's Your Skin Type?

Knowing your skin type can help you understand how to take care of your skin. Not all skin-care products and treatments are beneficial for all skin types. Take this test to determine your skin type, and then read on to learn how to help your particular skin look its best.

To begin, wash your face. Wait 2 hours and then examine your skin in the mirror.

Does your skin feel smooth, with no signs of flaking or oiliness?

You have normal/regular skin.

Does your skin feel slick and look shiny?
Does your face tend to break out often?

You have oily skin.

Does your skin feel tight and look flaky or scaly in some areas?
Do you tend to reach for moisturizer frequently?

You have dry skin.

Does your skin have a little bit of everything described above?

You have combination skin.

Does your skin look red and inflamed in some areas?
Does it feel irritated when it's first washed, even if it calms down later?

You have sensitive skin.

Before using a new ingredient on your face, always test it on the inside of your arm to see if it gives your skin an adverse reaction.

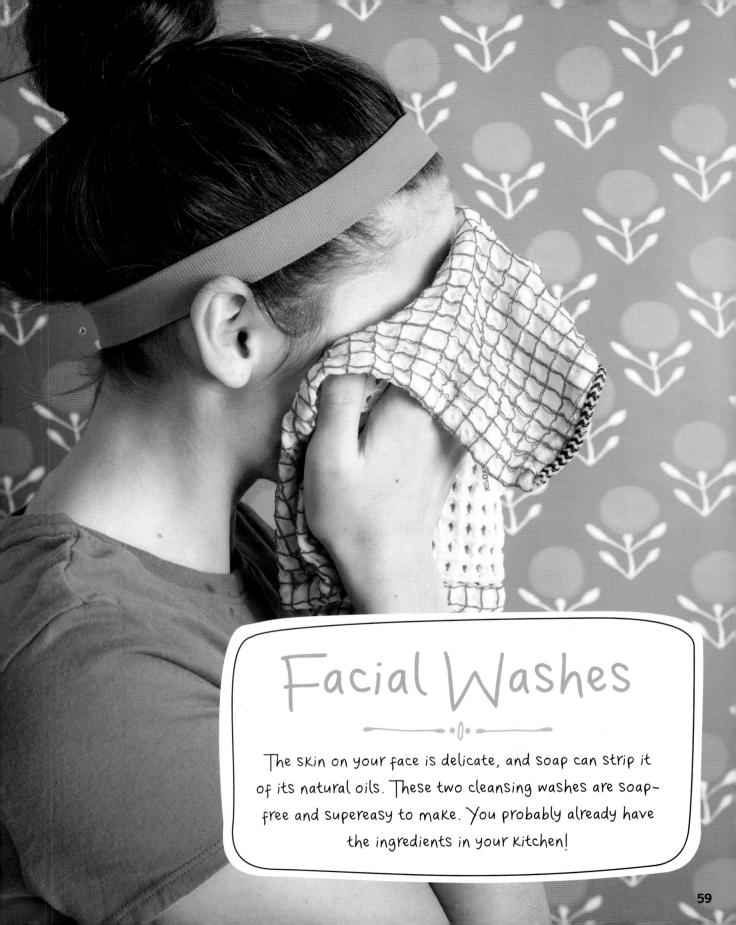

Facial Washes

The skin on your face is delicate, and soap can strip it of its natural oils. These two cleansing washes are soap-free and supereasy to make. You probably already have the ingredients in your kitchen!

OIL-AWAY CLEANSER

MAKES ¼ CUP

This cleanser is great for all skin types, even oily skin! It may sound crazy to put oil on already-oily skin, but it actually helps: oil dissolves oil. Coconut oil is solid at room temperature, but this cleanser will soften as it warms in your hands and on your face. You can use this cleanser every day.

WHAT YOU NEED

2 **tablespoons coconut oil**

2 **tablespoons olive oil**

HOW YOU MAKE IT

1. If the coconut oil is solid, melt it in a microwave or a double boiler. Then combine both oils in a bowl and blend with a spoon.

2. Transfer your mixture to a clean jar. Keep it at your bathroom sink.

HOW YOU USE IT

1. With clean hands, rub about 1 teaspoon of the cleanser between your palms to warm it. Gently massage it into your face, using small circular motions, for about a minute.

2. Wet a washcloth with hot water and wring out the excess water. Place the washcloth over your whole face to help unclog your pores.

3. After a few seconds, use the washcloth to wipe away the oil.

4. Rinse your face with cool water.

HONEY TAPPING

MAKES 1 APPLICATION

Honey naturally draws moisture to the skin. This cleanser is a one-ingredient dream product that you can use every day whatever your skin type.

WHAT YOU NEED

1–2 teaspoons raw honey

HOW YOU USE IT

1. Spread the honey all over your face.

2. Gently tap your fingers, as if you were typing on a keyboard, over the whole surface of your face. Continue until your fingertips are so tacky and sticky that they seem to stick to your skin.

3. Rinse your face and hands with warm water.

Toners

Toners are water-based liquids that soothe the skin, restore its pH balance, and smooth its surface. They also remove any traces of dirt, oil, and makeup that your cleanser may have missed. So go get some cotton balls and whip up the batch that's just right for you.

HYDRATING FLORAL TONER

MAKES ½ CUP

This sweet-smelling mixture can be used once a day and works well on regular-to-dry skin. Rosewater soothes irritated skin and refines pores without depleting moisture.

HOW YOU MAKE IT

1. Combine the rosewater, witch hazel, vinegar, and essential oil in a glass measuring cup with spout. Mix well with a spoon or whisk.

2. Transfer the blended liquid to a small bottle with a lid for storage.

HOW YOU USE IT

Cleanse your face. Then apply a small amount of the toner to a cotton ball and wipe gently all over your face.

WHAT YOU NEED

¼ cup rosewater

+

2 tablespoons witch hazel

+

1 teaspoon apple cider vinegar

+

8 drops lavender essential oil

APPLE-A-DAY TONER

MAKES 1 CUP

This easy-to-make toner is especially helpful for keeping oily skin clear and blemish-free. The apple cider vinegar kills bacteria and gets rid of excess oil and dirt while also dissolving dead skin cells.

WHAT YOU NEED

¼ cup apple cider vinegar (raw)

¾ cup distilled or purified water

HOW YOU MAKE IT

1. Combine the vinegar and water in a glass measuring cup with a spout. Mix well with a spoon or whisk.

2. Transfer the blended mixture to a small bottle with a lid for storage.

HOW YOU USE IT

Cleanse your face. Then apply a small amount of the toner to a cotton ball and wipe gently all over your face.

GREEN TEA TONER

MAKES ⅔ CUP

This blend is great to use daily for normal and combination skin because the ingredients complement each other so well. Green tea gently reduces oil production and makes pores appear smaller, and witch hazel alleviates irritation and inflammation. Aloe vera provides a moisture-retaining protective layer for the skin.

WHAT YOU NEED

- 2 **green tea bags**
- ½ **cup distilled or purified water**
- 1 **tablespoon aloe vera gel**
- 1 **tablespoon witch hazel**

HOW YOU MAKE IT

1. Make tea: Place the tea bags in a glass measuring cup with a spout. Heat the water over high heat until it is almost — but not quite — boiling. Pour the hot water over the tea bags and let steep for 10 minutes. Then remove the tea bags and let the tea cool to room temperature.

2. Add the aloe vera gel and witch hazel to the tea and stir until thoroughly combined.

3. Transfer the mixture to a small bottle with a lid for storage.

HOW YOU USE IT

Cleanse your face. Then apply a small amount of the toner to a cotton ball and wipe gently all over your face.

BASIC FACIAL SCRUB: THREE WAYS

MAKES 1 APPLICATION

Facial scrubs remove dead skin cells and make way for new ones. This process, called exfoliation, helps keep your complexion clear and radiant. It's best to exfoliate only once or twice a week so the delicate skin on your face doesn't get irritated. If you have sensitive skin, exfoliate very gently, making sure you never actually scrub your skin.

Here are three versions of a basic facial scrub formula. Choose the one that works best for your skin.

Sensitive and Dry Skin

Oily Skin

Normal and Combination Skin

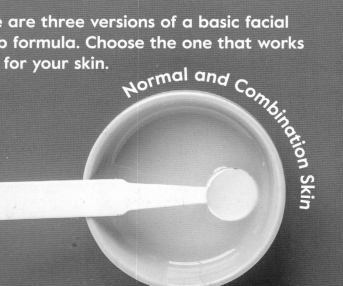

WHAT YOU NEED

Normal and Combination Skin

2 teaspoons coconut oil, warmed until liquid

1 teaspoon baking soda

Sensitive and Dry Skin

2 teaspoons raw honey

1 teaspoon oat flour or ground rolled oats

Oily Skin

2 teaspoons aloe vera gel

1 teaspoon baking soda

HOW YOU MAKE IT

Combine your ingredients in a small bowl and stir with a spoon until blended.

HOW YOU USE IT

1. Cleanse your face and rinse with warm water.

2. Gently apply the scrub to your face with your fingers, massaging it over your skin with small circular motions for about a minute. Avoid the delicate skin close to your eyes.

3. Rinse with cool water, making sure your face is clear of all the scrub particles, and pat your face dry.

Skin-Softening Steamer

Facial steaming helps unclog your pores to release dirt, oil, bacteria, and other toxins. The process also softens your skin. If you have extremely sensitive skin, though, you should avoid facial steams, because the heat can irritate your skin.

WHAT YOU NEED

+ 4–5 cups water
+ Tea kettle or large pot
+ 2 large towels
+ Large ceramic bowl
+ 1 mint tea bag
+ 1 chamomile tea bag

HOW YOU MAKE IT

1. Bring the water to boil in a large pot.

2. In the meantime, set up a steaming station at your kitchen table. Fold one of the towels and place it on the table. Set the bowl on top of it. Place the tea bags in the bowl.

3. When the water is boiling, carefully pour it into the bowl.

HOW YOU USE IT

1. Sit down at the table and lean over the bowl. Drape the second towel over both your head and the bowl to trap the steam.

2. Steam for about 10 minutes. Keep your face close enough to the bowl so that you feel the steam, but not so close that the steam burns you. The steam should feel relaxing, not painful.

3. When you're ready, take off the towel and go splash cool water over your face.

Blackhead Bulletin

Your body is covered in millions of hair follicles. Each follicle contains a gland that produces a kind of oil called sebum that helps keep your skin soft. Dead skin cells and excess oils can collect in your hair follicles and turn into tiny dark plugs that we call blackheads.

During puberty, your hormones are producing more oil than they used to. This makes your skin especially prone to blackheads, particularly on the T-zone, the central part of the face that includes the forehead, nose, and chin. So if you suddenly have more blackheads than you used to, don't worry! Now that you know what they are, you can take the first step to minimizing them: keeping your skin clean.

T-zone Strips

Keep your face clean, exfoliate regularly, and use these homemade strips once or twice a week to minimize blackheads. When this mixture dries and hardens, the astringent combination will draw out impurities. Give yourself a facial steam first (page 68) to allow any blackheads to lift out more easily.

WHAT YOU NEED

+ 1 egg

+ 1 squeeze of lemon juice

+ 2- by 3-inch strips of paper towel

WHAT YOU DO

1. Crack the egg open and separate the white from the yolk. Set the white in a bowl, and put the yolk in a container in the fridge for tomorrow's breakfast.

2. Add the lemon juice to the egg white and whisk until frothy.

3. Dip a paper towel strip in the egg mixture until it is just damp. Lay the moistened paper towel strip over your nose. Use more strips as necessary on any other part of your T-zone that has clogged pores.

4. Let the paper towels dry until they feel stiff to the touch, about 15 minutes. Then gently peel them off.

5. Splash your face with cool water and pat dry.

Facial Masks

Facial masks have super-powers! They draw out dirt and oil, make pores appear smaller, smooth and exfo-liate, and help nutrients soak deeply into the skin. They have other benefits, too, depending on the ingredients you use. And as a bonus, because you'll need to lie down to let the mask do its magic, you get to take a little break. The result is a smoother and brighter face and a more peaceful mood.

GREEN GODDESS HYDRATING MASK

MAKES 1 TREATMENT

If you have dry, flaky patches on your face, this mixture will quench your thirsty skin with superhydrating coconut milk and avocado. The spirulina nourishes all skin types. Before you mix up this mask, prepare a comfy place where you can lie down for a bit.

WHAT YOU NEED

¼ cup coconut milk

¼ avocado

⅛ teaspoon spirulina

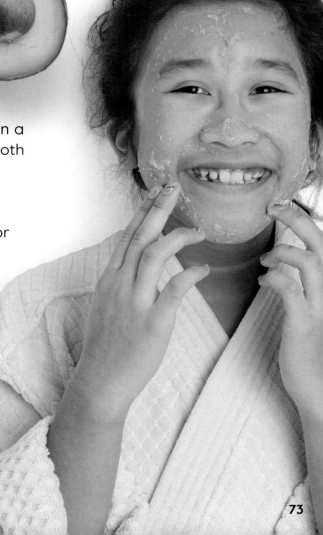

HOW YOU MAKE IT

Combine the coconut milk, avocado, and spirulina in a small bowl. Mash with a fork and blend until a smooth paste is formed.

HOW YOU USE IT

1. Cleanse your face, but don't apply any toner or moisturizer afterward.

2. Using your fingers, apply a light and even layer of the mask all over your face. Avoid the delicate skin around your eyes.

3. Set a timer for 15 to 20 minutes, then lie down. Relax.

4. When your timer goes off, rinse your face with warm water. Pat your face dry, then apply toner and moisturizer.

COMBO EGG MASK

MAKES 1 TREATMENT

Egg whites and yolks have different properties: the whites remove excess oil, while yolks add moisture. If you have combination skin, you can separate an egg and use each part to treat different conditions in different areas. Before you mix up this mask, prepare a comfy place where you can lie down for a bit.

WHAT YOU NEED

1 egg   +   Squeeze of lemon juice   +   1 teaspoon raw honey

HOW YOU MAKE IT

1. Separate the egg, placing the yolk in one bowl and the white in another bowl.

2. Add the lemon juice to the egg white. Whisk until frothy.

3. Add the honey to the egg yolk. Stir until smooth.

HOW YOU USE IT

1. Cleanse your face, but don't apply any toner or moisturizer afterward.

2. Using your fingers, apply a light and even layer of the egg white mixture on your T-zone and any other oily areas. Cover the rest of your face with the egg yolk mixture. Avoid the delicate skin around your eyes.

3. Set a timer for 15 to 20 minutes, then lie down. Relax.

4. When your timer goes off, rinse your face with warm water. Pat your face dry, then apply toner and moisturizer.

SHINE
BRIGHT

GOLDEN BRIGHTENING MASK

MAKES 1 TREATMENT

This mask works wonders to even out skin tone, prevent breakouts, and soothe blotchy skin. Turmeric, yogurt, and lemon all have mild bleaching effects, while the vinegar and honey heal and deeply clean your skin. Before you mix up this mask, prepare a comfy place where you can lie down for a bit.

WHAT YOU NEED

- 1 tablespoon raw honey
- 1 teaspoon apple cider vinegar
- ½ teaspoon yogurt
- ¼ teaspoon ground turmeric
- Squeeze of lemon juice

HOW YOU MAKE IT

Combine the honey, vinegar, yogurt, turmeric, and lemon juice in a small dish. Stir into a thick paste.

HOW YOU USE IT

1. Cleanse your face, but don't apply any toner or moisturizer afterward.

2. Using your fingers, apply a light and even layer of your mask all over your face, avoiding the delicate skin around your eyes.

3. Set a timer for 15 to 20 minutes, then lie down. Relax.

4. When your timer goes off, rinse your face with warm water. Pat your face dry, then apply toner and moisturizer.

DAY DREAM LOTION

MAKES ⅔ CUP

This amazing cream has everything your face needs for everyday moisturizing! If you double the recipe, you can keep one jar at home and another in your day bag for on-the-go moisturizing. Apply this cream lightly all over your face or just to the spots that need extra moisture.

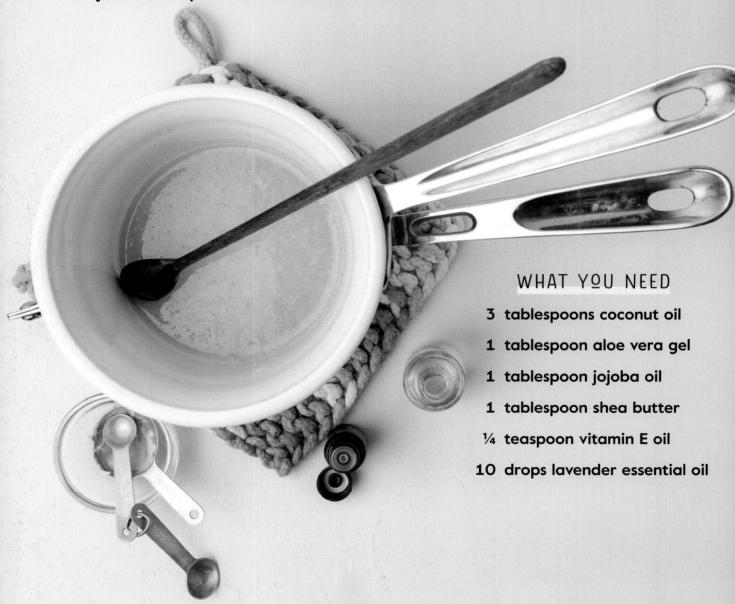

WHAT YOU NEED

3 tablespoons coconut oil

1 tablespoon aloe vera gel

1 tablespoon jojoba oil

1 tablespoon shea butter

¼ teaspoon vitamin E oil

10 drops lavender essential oil

HOW YOU MAKE IT

If the coconut oil is solid, melt it in a microwave or a double boiler.

Combine all the ingredients in a bowl. Using a hand mixer, whip until the cream is light and airy.

3 Transfer the lotion to a small glass jar. Store at room temperature, and use it up within a couple of weeks.

VEG OUT

If you're stressed out or overtired, chances are it's showing in your eyes. Maybe you have dark under-eye circles, or the skin around your eyes is dull or puffy. Both cucumbers and potatoes can refresh tired eyes, helping you look and feel energized. Potatoes have an additional superpower: they brighten and lighten dark circles. Relief is just around the corner — in your refrigerator!

Cuke Refresher

Place a thin slice of chilled cucumber on each eye, then sit back and relax until the cuke has reached room temperature, about 15 minutes.

Grater De-puffing Benefits

Finely grate about ¼ cup of cucumber, then chill it in the fridge for 20 minutes. Lie back, spread the specks evenly around your eyes, and relax. After about 15 minutes, remove the cucumber and rinse your face with cool water.

Potato to the Rescue

Cut two thin semicircles of potato. Slip one under each eye, then sit back and relax. After 15 minutes, remove the potatoes and rinse your face with cool water.

Miracle Mask

Grate equal amounts of cucumber and potato, mix well, and chill in the refrigerator for 20 minutes. Lie back and gently pat the mixture into place under your eyes. Leave on for 15 to 20 minutes, then remove the vegetables and rinse your face well with cool water.

SPA TIME=YOU TIME

Let yourself unwind by creating your very own spa experience at home. Gather all of your beauty products, several towels, slippers (page 145), and, of course, your robe! Let anyone else at home know that you won't be available for an hour or so. Dim the lights, put on some peaceful music, and begin relaxing!

1. **Cleanse** your face (page 59).

2. **Steam** to open up your pores (page 68).

3. **Exfoliate** (page 66).

4. **Apply a facial mask** or an eye mask (page 72) while you give yourself a relaxing foot soak (page 142).

5. **Soothe** your face with toner (page 62).

6. **Moisturize** (page 78). Always moisturize.

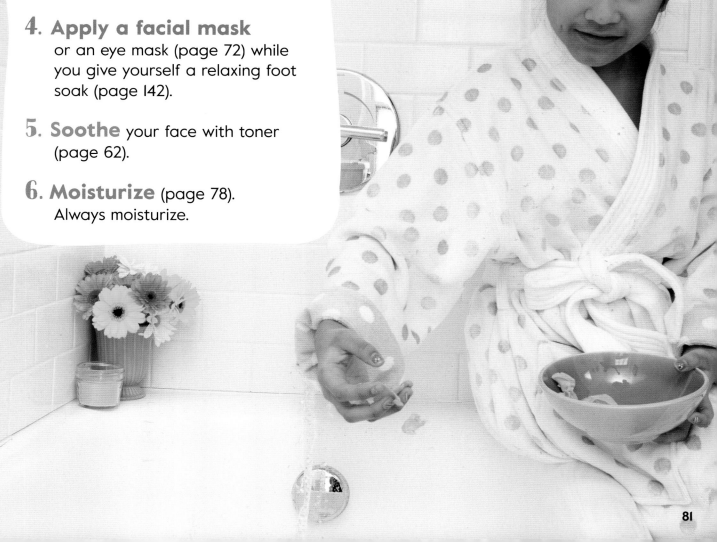

HAIR CARE

The beauty industry would like you to buy a whole shelf's worth of products to keep your hair shiny and manageable, but a few simple (and natural!) homemade products and techniques are all you really need to master your mane. All-natural shampoos are just the beginning. In this chapter, you'll also find instructions for hair masks, styling products, coloring methods, and even creative hair-styling techniques — because your hair is the one accessory you're always wearing!

Know Yourself

Healthy Hair 101

Luscious locks can be yours with just a little know-how. These basic hair-care tips will keep your tresses healthy and happy.

Wash your hair no more than every other day. When you do, use warm — not hot — water and massage your scalp to increase the blood flow.

If you have very dry or kinky hair, wash it no more than once a week. Use a conditioner instead of shampoo most of the time, and apply a hot oil treatment (page 93) once or twice a month to maintain your hair's moisture and elasticity.

Let your hair dry before combing or brushing it. Wet hair is more prone to breaking.

Use a wide-toothed comb to detangle your hair, working from the ends up to the scalp.

Avoid styling tools that use heat. See page 97 for ideas on creating waves without heat.

Pull your hair back with soft ponytail holders, which are less damaging than rubber bands.

Trim your hair every 6 to 8 weeks to avoid dry, damaged ends.

What's Your Hair Type?

Oily hair can look dull and limp. It often seems greasy even just a few hours after it's been washed. If your hair is oily, chances are you also have an oily scalp and dandruff. If you have oily skin, it's likely that your scalp will be oily, too, which can make your hair look greasy.

Dry hair is often frizzy, with frequent flyaways and split ends, and it easily breaks. If you have dry skin, most likely your hair will be dry also.

Normal hair might be the most uncommon hair type. Consider yourself lucky if your hair is shiny and manageable most of the time!

Shampoos

—— ◦◊◦ ——

Making your own shampoo will give you total control over what you're putting on your head, help save the planet from toxic ingredients, and save you money. Plus, it's fun and supereasy! Store your homemade shampoo in a plastic bottle; you can reuse a commercial shampoo bottle if you have one.

SHINE-ON SHAMPOO

MAKES 1¼ CUPS

This is a great all-around shampoo for normal hair. It will give your hair a nice gleam and also some body because it does not weigh down the hair shaft as commercial shampoos often do. Use it as you would your regular shampoo.

WHAT YOU NEED

- 1 cup liquid castile soap
- 1 tablespoon raw honey
- ¼ cup distilled or purified water
- 8 drops lavender or peppermint essential oil

HOW YOU MAKE IT

1. Combine all the ingredients in a small bowl and whisk together.

2. Transfer the mixture to a plastic squeeze bottle.

87

DANDRUFF-DISAPPEARING SHAMPOO

MAKES 2 CUPS

Did you know that dandruff often comes from having an oily scalp, not a dry one? This shampoo will take care of both problems, keeping your hair *and* scalp feeling superclean and flake-free. It won't lather like store-bought shampoo, but that doesn't mean this hardworking mixture isn't doing its job! Use it as you would your regular shampoo.

WHAT YOU NEED

2 cups hot distilled or purified water

1 tablespoon apple cider vinegar (raw)

½ tablespoon baking soda

8 drops tea tree essential oil

HOW YOU MAKE IT

1. Combine all the ingredients in a bowl and whisk together until the baking soda has dissolved.

2. Transfer the mixture to a plastic squeeze bottle.

CONDITIONING SHAMPOO

MAKES 1¼ CUPS

This supermoisturizing shampoo is the perfect remedy for dry hair. It's especially useful for swimmers, who need an extra boost of moisture to balance out the drying chlorine in pools. Use it as you would your regular shampoo.

WHAT YOU NEED

1 cup liquid castile soap

¼ cup coconut milk

1 teaspoon vitamin E oil

8 drops lavender essential oil

HOW YOU MAKE IT

1. Combine all the ingredients in a bowl and whisk together.

2. Transfer the mixture to a plastic squeeze bottle.

Hair Masks

When your hair and scalp need some extra moisture, masks can provide deep conditioning by soaking into the hair cuticles. Use one of these hair mask recipes once a month.

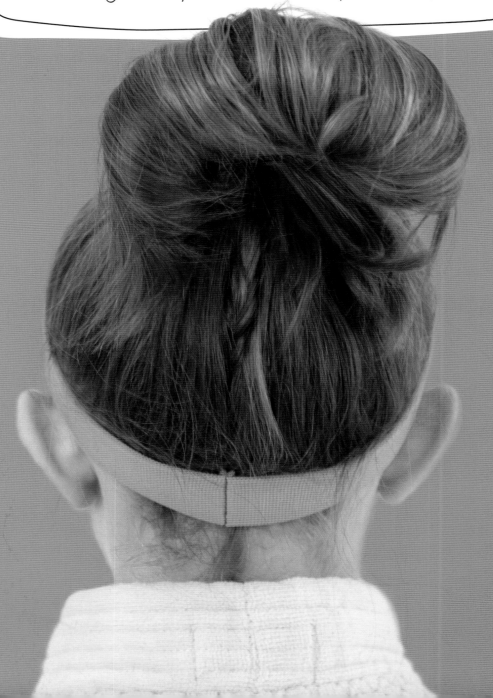

HONEY-YOGURT HAIR MASK

MAKES 1 TREATMENT

Keeping the pH of your scalp slightly acidic helps prevent your hair from getting dry, frizzy, or brittle. In this mask, yogurt and honey feed your scalp and balance its pH, while aloe vera stimulates hair growth. The olive oil gives your hair softness and shine.

WHAT YOU NEED

2½ tablespoons aloe vera gel

2 tablespoons olive oil

2 tablespoons plain yogurt

1 tablespoon raw honey

HOW YOU MAKE IT

1. Combine all the ingredients in a blender and blend until completely smooth.

2. Transfer the mixture to a plastic squeeze bottle.

HOW YOU USE IT

1. Rub the mixture into your scalp while your hair is dry.

2. Wrap your hair in a towel and let sit for 30 minutes.

3. Rinse the mixture out of your hair, and then shampoo as usual.

COCONUT-BANANA DEEP MOISTURE MASK

MAKES 1 TREATMENT

Bananas are loaded with vitamins your hair is hungry for, and coconut's fatty acids will make your tresses soft and silky.

WHAT YOU NEED

- 2 tablespoons coconut oil
- 1 medium banana (or 2 or even 3 if you have very long hair)
- 2 tablespoons coconut milk
- 2 tablespoons raw honey

HOW YOU MAKE IT

1. If the coconut oil is solid, melt it in a microwave or a double boiler.

2. Combine all the ingredients in a blender and blend until completely smooth.

3. Transfer the mixture to a plastic squeeze bottle.

HOW YOU USE IT

1. While your hair is dry, rub the mixture into your scalp and all the way down your hair.

2. Wrap your hair in a towel and let sit for 30 minutes.

3. Rinse the mixture out of your hair, and then shampoo as usual.

Hot Oil Treatment

Use this hot oil treatment to deliver deep moisture to very dry and brittle or kinky hair. The coconut oil seeps into the hair cuticle, while the jojoba oil seals in moisture. Washing your hair with a mild shampoo before applying this treatment will open up your hair's outermost layers and help the oil soak in.

WHAT YOU NEED

+ Large bowl

+ Small bowl

+ ⅓ cup coconut oil (more if you have a lot of hair)

+ 1 tablespoon jojoba oil

+ Plastic shower cap

+ Towel

HOW YOU MAKE IT

1. Fill a large bowl with hot water.

2. Combine the coconut oil and jojoba oil in a small bowl, then place that bowl in the hot water. Stir the oils until they are fully mixed and warm, but not so hot that they will burn your scalp.

HOW YOU USE IT

1. Coat your hair with the warm oil, working in sections and making sure the mixture soaks into the full length of your hair.

2. Cover your hair with a plastic shower cap.

3. Warm a towel in the microwave, wrap it around the shower cap, and leave on for 15 to 20 minutes.

4. Rinse the mixture out of your hair, but do not shampoo again.

5. Apply a conditioner and continue styling as usual.

Wrap It Up

Use an old T-shirt to make a quick and comfy no-sew head wrap that will keep every strand of hair out of your face and behind your shoulders. It's the perfect accessory for your facial cleansing routine!

WHAT YOU NEED

+ 1 large or extra-large short-sleeve T-shirt

+ Scissors

HOW YOU MAKE IT

1 Lay the shirt flat and smooth out one of the sleeves.

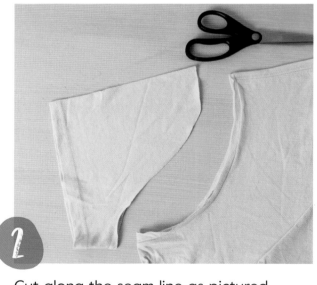

2 Cut along the seam line as pictured.

Slip on the cut-off sleeve as shown, with your hair flowing out.

DANDRUFF RINSE

MAKES 1 CUP

If you need immediate relief for your itchy scalp, try this rinse. Apple cider vinegar is antifungal, antibacterial, and anti-inflammatory, so it treats a variety of causes for an irritated scalp with one easy — and natural — routine. You can use it once or twice a week. Also try the Dandruff-Disappearing Shampoo (page 88), which may eliminate the flakes.

WHAT YOU NEED

½ cup apple cider vinegar (raw)

½ cup warm distilled or purified water

HOW YOU MAKE IT

Combine both ingredients in a spray bottle. Shake well.

HOW YOU USE IT

1. Spray onto your scalp until saturated.

2. Wrap a towel around your head and leave on for 30 minutes to 1 hour.

3. Rinse and then shampoo as usual.

ON-THE-GO DRY SHAMPOO

MAKES ¼ CUP

When your hair needs washing but you woke up too late for a shower, a dry shampoo is the perfect solution! It absorbs oils from the scalp, resulting in hair that's lighter and full of body.

WHAT YOU NEED

- **2 tablespoons arrowroot powder**
- **1 tablespoon bentonite clay**
- **5 drops lavender essential oil**

Note: If you have dark hair, add unsweetened cocoa powder to this mixture. Start with 2 teaspoons and add more if needed to match your hair color.

HOW YOU MAKE IT

1. Measure all the ingredients into a mixing bowl and blend lightly with a fork.

2. Transfer the mixture to a small bottle with a shaker cap.

HOW YOU USE IT

Shake a small amount of the powder onto the roots of your hair and massage in lightly. Wait a few minutes, and then brush and style your hair as you do regularly.

MAKE WAVES

If you were born with straight hair, creating curls and waves doesn't have to involve harsh chemicals and scorching irons. All you need is some creativity and a little planning. Turn the page for some fun ways to make your hair bounce!

Headband Waves

With your hair damp, slide a stretchy fabric headband around your forehead.

Separate out 2-inch sections of hair and wrap each one around the headband. Secure the end of each section between your head and the band. Go to sleep.

In the morning, unwrap the sections into beautiful curls.

Finger comb gently to maintain the waves and prevent frizz.

Bobby Spirals

Gather as many bobby pins as you can find, and get ready for sensational spirals!

Beginning at the ends, fold thin sections of damp hair up toward your scalp. Secure each finished section with a pin.

When your hair is dry, unravel your spiraled locks. You can do this at night before going to bed and wake up to lovely curls!

Mini Buns

This isn't comfy for sleeping, so start several hours before you want your hair to be ready.

Divide your damp hair into multiple 2-inch sections and twist each one into a tiny bun. Fasten a hair elastic around each bun right at your scalp.

Once your hair feels dry, let the buns loose and enjoy!

Rag Curls

This method was around long before curling irons — and before electricity!

Cut an old T-shirt into skinny strips. Divide your damp hair into thin sections. Wind each section tightly around a T-shirt strip. Knot the ends of the strip.

Once your hair is dry, untie and untwist the strips to reveal gorgeous waves.

ALOE VERA STYLING SPRAY

MAKES 1¼ CUPS

Use this spray as you would a traditional hair spray. The sugar adds a slightly stiff coating to hold a hairstyle in place. For the essential oil, use your favorite. I like lavender and rosemary because they smell nice and help nourish hair.

WHAT YOU NEED

2 tablespoons sugar

1 cup hot distilled or purified water

1 tablespoon aloe vera gel

1 tablespoon rubbing alcohol

6 drops essential oil

HOW YOU MAKE IT

1. Place the sugar in a bowl and pour in the hot water. Whisk until the sugar is dissolved. Let the mixture cool until it's warm to the touch but not hot, about 10 minutes.

2. Pour the sugar water into a spritzer bottle, add the rest of the ingredients, and shake well.

OCEAN SPRAY

MAKES 1 CUP

If you have straight hair, you've probably noticed that your hair gets wonderfully wavy and full after a day at the shore. With this spray, you can create that same wonderful texture without getting sand between your toes! Just remember that salt can dry out hair, so condition well before you spritz, and don't use this spray every day.

WHAT YOU NEED

- **1** cup hot distilled or purified water
- **2½** tablespoons sea salt
- **1** teaspoon aloe vera gel
- **½** teaspoon coconut oil

HOW YOU MAKE IT

Combine all the ingredients in a spray bottle and shake until thoroughly mixed.

HOW YOU USE IT

Spritz onto freshly washed, damp hair and scrunch with a towel. Keep scrunching with your hands as your hair dries.

DETANGLER SPRAY

MAKES 1 CUP

Don't let your tangles get the best of you. This spray helps smooth out hair shafts to loosen knots and snarls.

WHAT YOU NEED

¾ cup distilled or purified water

2 tablespoons aloe vera gel

2 tablespoons apple cider vinegar

10 drops lavender or rosemary essential oil

HOW YOU MAKE IT

Combine all the ingredients in a spray bottle and shake until mixed completely.

HOW YOU USE IT

Spritz liberally on wet or dry hair, then comb through.

LICE-AWAY SPRAY

MAKES ½ CUP

Use this spray each night during a lice outbreak or after possible exposure to keep bugs at bay. Tea tree and lavender essential oils work like magic to both kill lice and make your hair less appealing for them to hop into.

WHAT YOU NEED

½ cup distilled or purified water

15 drops tea tree essential oil

10 drops lavender essential oil

HOW YOU MAKE IT

Combine all the ingredients in a spray bottle and shake until thoroughly mixed.

HOW YOU USE IT

Spray your entire head each night, making sure to get behind your ears and the back of your neck. Comb the spray through your hair.

AVOID HEAD HOPPING

Never share brushes and hats with your friends. Be aware of and careful in the places where lice are likely to spread, like at school, camp, and sleepovers.

Color Streaking

Add some temporary rainbows to your hair with supplies from your local art store. Pastels may be fun on paper, but they are even more exciting when painted onto sections of your hair! These color streaks will wash out completely after two or three shampoos, so it's an enjoyable way to have short-term experiments with colors and patterns. Use nontoxic art pastels.

WHAT YOU NEED

+ Art pastels

+ Spray bottle filled with water

+ Aloe Vera Styling Spray (page 100), optional

TRY THIS

Use different colors from the roots to the ends, paint in stripes framing your face, or perhaps just color the tips of your hair.

For darker hair, reds and purples work best.

Lighter hair can handle blues and greens with ease.

NO-STRESS MESS

This colorful project can get messy, so cover any nearby surfaces with paper towels or rags and have an extra rag ready for wiping your hands. Set up in front of a mirror with a comb or brush that you don't mind getting dyed with color. Wrap an old towel around your shoulders to protect your shirt.

HOW YOU DO IT

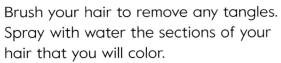

1 Brush your hair to remove any tangles. Spray with water the sections of your hair that you will color.

2 Hold the wet section of hair away from your head with your free hand. Paint the hair in downward strokes with the pastel.

3 Repeat steps 1 and 2 for as much of your hair as you want to color. Let your hair air-dry and then brush it. Add a spritz of hairspray to help set the color, if you like.

BODY-CARE CONCOCTIONS

Your face tends to get the most attention in your skin-care routine, but it's important to give the rest of your body love and care, too. This chapter has everything you need for healthy and sweet-smelling skin from head to toe — from luscious body butters to fruity shower scrubs to natural deodorant you can make yourself!

Body-Care Tips

Through your preteen and teen years, your changing body needs special care. Hormone surges mean you sweat more, which can make it hard to smell fresh all day. Often, your skin also becomes more oily, and not just on your face; it's common for pimples to break out on your back and chest, too. Here are five ways to ensure your whole body feels — and smells — its best.

Shower every day using a gentle cleanser to keep pimples and body odor away.

Apply lotion right after a shower while your skin is still damp to lock in moisture in places that get dry and itchy, like your elbows, knees, and legs.

Rinse off after playing sports or exercising.

Use deodorant daily to maintain the results of washing regularly.

Wash your clothes, towels, and sheets regularly. Fabric holds on to odors and oils, so toss items that come in contact with your body into the hamper! Wear a fresh shirt every day. Hang up your towel after you shower. And change your sheets weekly.

TOO-GOOD BODY BUTTER

MAKES 1 CUP

This is unlike any lotion you've tried before, and with only two magic ingredients, it's almost too good to be true! It spreads on like a cloud and then instantly dissolves into your skin without leaving any greasiness. Use it all over your body to feel velvety soft. This butter stays fresh for several months, much longer than most other whole-foods beauty products. It makes an awesome gift!

WHAT YOU NEED

⅔ cup cocoa butter

⅓ cup coconut oil

HOW YOU MAKE IT

1. Combine the cocoa butter and coconut oil in a double boiler and melt over low heat.

2. Remove from the stove. Mix lightly with a spoon, then scrape the mixture into a bowl. Set in the refrigerator to cool.

3. Once the mixture has solidified slightly *but is still soft* — about 5 minutes — remove it from the refrigerator. Using a mixer with a whisk attachment, whip it into fluffy clouds.

4. Transfer to a clean jar, cover, and enjoy!

SUNSHINE BARS

They look like soap but act like lotion! These little moisturizing bars travel well, so throw one or two into a tin and bring them wherever you roam. Keep one in a dish in your bathroom and rub it on your warm skin after every shower or bath. You can easily multiply the recipe and make a big batch for all of your friends!

WHAT YOU NEED

- ¼ cup beeswax
- ¼ cup cocoa butter
- ¼ cup coconut oil
- 5 drops lemon essential oil
- 5 drops orange essential oil

HOW YOU MAKE IT

1. Combine the beeswax, cocoa butter, and coconut oil in a double boiler. Melt over low heat, stirring with a whisk.

2. Remove from the heat. Add the essential oils, stirring gently.

3. Carefully pour the mixture into ice cube trays.

4. Let cool completely to room temperature for a couple of hours or overnight. Then pop out the cubes and store in tins or jars.

SWEET-SMELLING DEODORANT STICK

MAKES 1 STICK

Making your own all-natural deodorant is easy and the result is effective. Use it as you would your regular deodorant. This recipe is wonderful for sensitive skin and conveniently fits in most deodorant tubes; find a new one online, or sterilize and reuse one you already have.

WHAT YOU NEED

- ¼ cup cocoa butter
- 1½ tablespoons beeswax
- 4 teaspoons bentonite clay
- 10 drops lavender essential oil
- 10 drops tea tree essential oil

HOW YOU MAKE IT

1. Combine the cocoa butter and beeswax in a double boiler and melt over low heat.

2. Add the bentonite clay and mix with a spoon until combined.

3. Remove from the heat and add the essential oils, stirring gently.

4. Pour the mixture into an empty deodorant tube. Let stand for a few hours or overnight, until cooled to room temperature.

5. When the deodorant stick is fully cool, cap it.

To Shave or Not to Shave

We all have hair on our bodies, and as you go through puberty, it gets darker and thicker and grows in new places. The most important thing to know about body hair is that it's completely natural, whether you have a little or a lot.

Like many girls, you may feel self-conscious about hair on your legs, in your armpits, or peeking out from your bathing suit. Throughout our lives, we get messages from media and society that encourage that sense of embarrassment. But your choices about keeping or removing your hair are entirely personal. You should make that decision for yourself! Don't let anyone pressure you to make a choice you're not ready to make. It's your body and no one else's!

If you are interested in removing your body hair, shaving is the most affordable and natural option. It also has the benefit of letting your hair grow back in a few days if you ever change your mind.

MYTH BUSTER: Shaving does *not* make your hair grow back faster and thicker. Regrowing hair only appears to be thicker because its ends are blunt after being cut by the razor.

Know Yourself
Shaving Guide

Whether you've tried shaving before or it's your very first time, these tips will make the process *smooth!*

Always wet your skin first. Use water and soap or shaving cream (see the recipe on page 114). This will minimize irritation to your skin.

Shave in the direction opposite of hair growth. For legs this means shaving upward. For armpits, try shaving in each direction: up, down, and side to side.

A light stroke is always best, especially around tricky spots like your ankles and knees, to avoid cutting yourself.

Exfoliate skin every few days and right before shaving with scrubs or a washcloth. This will minimize ingrown hairs, which can create little pimple-like bumps. Who needs another pimple?

Use a clean and sharp blade. Rinse your razor after every use and let it air-dry. Dull razors = cuts and nicks. Change your blades regularly.

SILKY-SMOOTH SHAVING CREAM

MAKES ½ CUP

Keep this cream on hand for silky-smooth skin and a close shave. Be careful in the shower when you're using it, as it can make the floor of the shower slippery. In a tub, an anti-skid mat can be helpful. Store this cream in a cool, dry place, and try to keep water out of the jar to preserve its freshness.

WHAT YOU NEED

¼ **cup coconut oil**

¼ **cup shea butter**

HOW YOU MAKE IT

1. If the coconut oil is solid, melt it in a microwave or a double boiler.

2. Combine the coconut oil and shea butter in a bowl. Using an electric mixer, whip until light and fluffy, about 2 minutes.

3. Scrape the cream with a spatula into a glass jar with a lid.

SMOOTH

HOW YOU USE IT

At the end of a shower or bath — when your skin and hair are softer — spread a dollop on your armpits, legs, or anywhere else you're shaving. Shave with gentle strokes in the direction opposite of hair growth. Rinse off the razor blade as you go.

Bee Candles

It's so easy and fun to make this little candle — and it smells great! Draw a bath, dim the lights, and soak in this candle's mild fragrance as you relax in the tub. You may even already have beeswax, the main ingredient, since many of the recipes in this book use it. If you have a large pot and small jars you can make several candles at a time.

WHAT YOU NEED

+ Small jelly jars

+ Beeswax

+ Shallow pan

+ Essential oil of choice, for fragrance (optional)

+ Toothpick (optional)

+ Wicks (available at most craft stores)

+ Pencil

HOW YOU MAKE IT

Fill the jars halfway with beeswax. If your beeswax came in a large chunk, you'll want to chop it into small pieces before filling the jar.

2

Carefully place the jars in a shallow pan of water on the stove. Heat slowly until the wax has completely melted.

3

Remove each jar from the heat. Add a few drops of essential oil to the melted wax, if desired. Stir briefly with a toothpick.

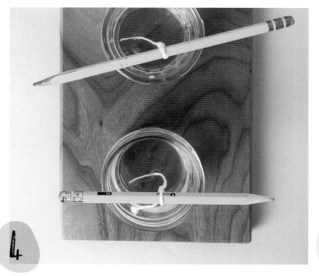

4

Dangle one end of the wick down into the wax. The bottom of the wick should touch the bottom of the jar. Tie the other end of the wick to the middle of a pencil, and lay the pencil over the jar rim so the wick is centered in the jar. Trim the extra wick above the knot on the pencil so it doesn't dangle back down into the jar.

5

Let cool overnight. Then remove the pencil and cut the wick about ½ inch above the cooled wax.

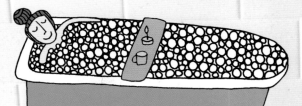

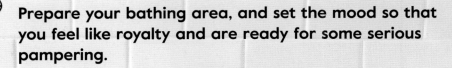

BATHE LIKE A GODDESS

Prepare your bathing area, and set the mood so that you feel like royalty and are ready for some serious pampering.

+ Set up a playlist of soft music.

+ Clear clutter off any surfaces.

+ Place a bouquet of flowers in the bathroom.

+ Have a glass of chilled juice or hot tea at the ready.

+ Fill your bathtub, and add flower petals and a few drops of lavender essential oil to the bathwater.

+ Lay out a fresh towel within reach of the bath.

+ Set a stool or chair beside the tub if you need an extra table surface. Place a tray on it with bath treats like the Rose Bath Balls (page 121) and Calming Salt Scrub (page 122).

+ Light a couple of Bee Candles (page 116).

+ Get in and relax.

Skin-Soothing Oat Bath Bag

Oats have been used for centuries to relieve itchy and irritated skin. In the bath, they are the perfect remedy for dry skin, eczema, or even a rash caused by heat or poison ivy! Use this simple bath bag to soften rough spots like elbows, knees, and heels and to give your entire body a smooth finish.

WHAT YOU NEED

+ ½ cup instant or rolled oats

+ Clean, thin crew sock

HOW YOU MAKE IT

1. Pour the oats into a blender and chop to a fine powder.

2. Pour the powdered oats into the sock and tie a knot at the top of the sock.

3. Drop the bath bag into the tub while you fill it with warm water.

4. As you bathe, squeeze the bath bag and rub it gently over your skin.

5. When your bath is over, discard the oats and rinse out your sock so that you can use it again next time.

Tub Tea

Step into your own giant cup of tea! Transform an ordinary bath by tossing in two or three tea bags as the tub fills up. Try a minty variety like peppermint or spearmint to recharge and energize. Or steep in tranquility, and quiet your mind with chamomile tea.

ROSE BATH BALLS

Settle into a hot bath with one of these fizzy pink spheres and let scents of rose and lavender fill the air while your everyday cares melt away. You can buy bath bomb molds online, or just roll out balls with your hands. If you go the hand-rolled route, you may need to add a drop or two of water to your mixture.

WHAT YOU NEED

- 1 **cup baking soda**
- ½ **cup citric acid**
- ½ **cup Epsom salt or sea salt**
- ¼ **cup cornstarch**
- 1 **tablespoon dried rose petals**
- 2 **teaspoons beet powder**
- 2½ **tablespoons coconut oil**
- 12 **drops lavender essential oil**

HOW YOU MAKE IT

1. Combine the baking soda, citric acid, Epsom salt, cornstarch, rose petals, and beet powder in a bowl and mix with a fork.

2. If the coconut oil is solid, melt it in a microwave or a double boiler. Combine the coconut oil and essential oil in a medium bowl and blend with a whisk.

3. Slowly pour the dry ingredients into the wet ingredients, stirring with a spoon and then your hands until the mixture feels like crumbly wet sand.

4. Pack the mixture into your molds, or roll by hand into 1-inch balls. Set them on a tray lined with parchment paper.

5. Let the balls dry for 24 hours. Once they're completely dry, store them in an airtight container.

WATCH YOUR STEP

Take extra care whenever you use these bath balls in the tub, since the oil they contain can make the tub slippery!

CALMING SALT SCRUB

MAKES ½ CUP

The mineral-rich salts in this scrub relax your muscles while casting off dead skin cells. Soothing floral scents will ease your busy mind, and the coconut oil adds moisture to your fresh layer of skin. Store this scrub in an airtight jar near your tub.

WHAT YOU NEED

¼ **cup coconut oil**

¼ **cup fine sea salt**

6 **drops lavender or rose essential oil**

Sprinkle of dried and crushed rose petals

HOW YOU MAKE IT

1. If the coconut oil is solid, melt it in a microwave or a double boiler.

2. Combine the coconut oil with the remaining ingredients in a glass jar and mix well with a spoon.

HOW YOU USE IT

After soaking in a warm bath for a while, gently rub the scrub all over your skin. Keep soaking in the bath while the scrub melts into the water.

WATCH YOUR STEP

Take extra care whenever you use this scrub in the tub, since the oils it contains can make the tub slippery!

STRAWBERRIES & CREAM SHOWER SCRUB

MAKES ¾ CUP

Transform your shower into a summer day with this dessert for your skin. It polishes, brightens, and moisturizes — all while smelling divine. This scrub does not store well, so make it right before you plan to use it.

WHAT YOU NEED

- **3 fresh strawberries, stems removed**
- **3 tablespoons coconut oil**
- **½ cup sugar**
- **1 teaspoon lemon juice**
- **3 drops lemon essential oil**

HOW YOU MAKE IT

1. Mash the strawberries in a small bowl with a fork until smooth.

2. If the coconut oil is solid, melt it in a microwave or a double boiler.

3. Add the coconut oil, sugar, lemon juice, and essential oil to the mashed strawberries, and whisk until fully combined.

HOW YOU USE IT

At the end of your shower, slather the scrub all over your body. Rinse well.

WATCH YOUR STEP

Take extra care whenever you use this scrub, since the oils it contains can make the shower floor slippery!

SPA GIFTS

Your homemade beauty products make fabulous gifts! Create double and triple batches of your favorite formulas and package them up in trios as presents for friends and family. Here are some combinations that go together well.

Bath Basket: Sunshine Bars (page 110), Rose Bath Balls (page 121), and Calming Salt Scrub (page 122).

Facial Basket: Apple-a-Day Toner (page 64), Basic Facial Scrub: Three Ways (page 66), and Mint Chip Lip Balm (page 128).

Sleep Basket: Sleep Tight Tea (page 20), Lavender Sleep Mask (page 23), and Sweet Dreams Spray (page 27).

Hands and Feet Basket: Nourishing Cuticle Oil (page 134), Moisturizing Hand Scrub (page 136), Healing Heel Stick (page 143), and a printed copy of the foot reflexology chart (page 149).

Know Yourself

Happy Smiles

Nothing is more contagious than a big, bright smile! Take care of your mouth and teeth with good oral hygiene. Here are six tips to keep you grinning:

Brush your teeth at least twice a day.

Use a soft toothbrush, which is gentler on teeth and gums.

Set a timer for 2 minutes to make sure you brush thoroughly.

Brush your gum line in addition to your teeth. Also brush the surface of your tongue and the roof of your mouth to remove bacteria.

Floss once a day. It's a chore and so easy to skip. Don't! Flossing removes food particles that brushing can't.

Schedule dental checkups and cleanings twice a year.

TOOTHPASTE

FLOSS DAILY

2 MIN.

BERRY WHITE TOOTH WHITENER

Are you brushing and flossing every day but still feel like your teeth aren't as bright as you'd like? Try using strawberries, whose acids have natural bleaching power! Store any leftover whitening paste in the refrigerator, where it will keep for up to 2 days.

WHAT YOU NEED

- 1 strawberry, stem removed
- 1 teaspoon baking soda
- 3 drops lemon essential oil

HOW YOU MAKE IT

1. Mash the strawberry in a small bowl with a fork until smooth.

2. Add the baking soda and blend with the fork until a smooth paste forms.

3. Add the essential oil and stir until fully mixed.

HOW YOU USE IT

1. Dip your toothbrush into the mixture, then use it to brush your teeth for 1 to 2 minutes.

2. Rinse your mouth well with water, then brush your teeth again with your regular toothpaste.

SUGAR & SPICE LIP SCRUB

MAKES ⅛ CUP

A lip scrub is a great remedy for chapped lips. You'll exfoliate dead skin cells while moisturizing, and the cinnamon naturally plumps up your lips by gently stimulating the skin and making it swell slightly. Store this mixture at your bathroom sink; it will keep for a couple of weeks.

WHAT YOU NEED

1 tablespoon coconut oil

2 teaspoons sugar

1 teaspoon raw honey

Dash of ground cinnamon

HOW YOU MAKE IT

1. If the coconut oil is solid, melt it in a microwave or a double boiler.

2. Combine the coconut oil with the remaining ingredients in a small bowl and blend thoroughly.

3. Transfer the scrub to a small container with a lid.

HOW YOU USE IT

After brushing your teeth, scoop a little of this scrub onto your fingers and massage it onto your lips. Rinse off with warm water.

MINT CHIP LIP BALM

MAKES ¼ CUP

This delicious treat will protect and moisturize your lips while smelling good enough to eat!

WHAT YOU NEED

1½ tablespoons coconut oil

1 tablespoon beeswax

1 tablespoon cocoa butter

½ teaspoon cocoa powder

5 drops peppermint essential oil

HOW YOU MAKE IT

1. Combine the coconut oil, beeswax, cocoa butter, and cocoa powder in a double boiler. Warm over low heat, stirring gently, until the fats have melted and the ingredients are thoroughly mixed.

2. Remove from the heat and stir in the essential oil.

3. Carefully pour the hot mixture into tins, tubes, or small jars.

4. Let the lip balm cool overnight before capping.

JUST BE YOU

PINK LEMONADE GLOSS

MAKES ¼ CUP

Shine and a hint of color make this a fun way to moisturize your lips for special occasions. You can find beet powder at most health food stores.

WHAT YOU NEED

- **2 tablespoons almond oil**
- **1 tablespoon beeswax**
- **1 tablespoon shea butter**
- **½ teaspoon beet powder**
- **5 drops lemon essential oil**

HOW YOU MAKE IT

1. Combine the almond oil, beeswax, and shea butter in a double boiler. Warm over low heat, stirring gently, until the fats have melted.

2. Remove from the heat and stir in the beet powder and essential oil.

3. Whisk the mixture for about a minute as it cools and thickens to keep the beet powder blended.

4. While the mixture is still slightly warm, carefully pour it into tins or tiny jars.

5. Let the lip gloss cool overnight before capping.

HEALTHY HANDS & FEET

Keeping your nails clean and well groomed is a quiet but very public statement about how you take care of yourself. Your fingernails and toenails can also be a wonderful expression of your mood and personality if you choose to decorate them. Your feet take you everywhere and rarely complain. Give them the attention they deserve with a good scrubbing, a satisfying soak, and some healing moisture. They'll thank you, for sure!

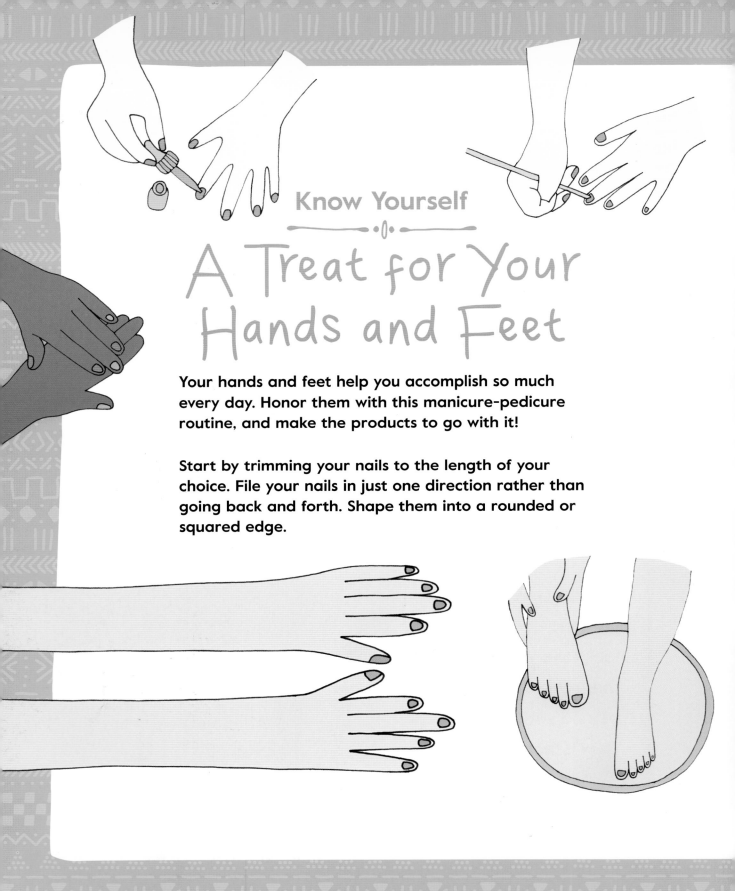

Know Yourself

A Treat for Your Hands and Feet

Your hands and feet help you accomplish so much every day. Honor them with this manicure-pedicure routine, and make the products to go with it!

Start by trimming your nails to the length of your choice. File your nails in just one direction rather than going back and forth. Shape them into a rounded or squared edge.

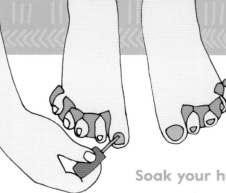

Hands

Soak your hands in the Sparkle Nail Soak (page 135).

Soften your cuticles by massaging the Nourishing Cuticle Oil (page 134) into your nails and nail beds.

Push your cuticles back very gently while they are soft and moisturized.

Exfoliate your hands with the Moisturizing Hand Scrub (page 136), then rinse in warm water.

Shine your nails with a soft buffer.

Moisturize your hands with the Extra-Rich Hand Cream (page 137).

Polish your nails (page 138), if desired.

Feet

Soak your feet in the Fizzy Foot Soak (page 142).

Exfoliate using the Zesty Foot Scrub (page 141) while the foot-soak water is still warm. Pat your feet dry.

Moisturize with your favorite cream — the Extra-Rich Hand Cream (page 137) can do double duty on your feet!

Polish your nails (page 138), if desired.

NOURISHING CUTICLE OIL

MAKES 1-2 TREATMENTS

Cuticles act as a barrier to help protect your nail roots. Keeping them soft and healthy is all the care they need. Cutting them can lead to infections. Massage this oil into your cuticles and nail beds several times a week.

WHAT YOU NEED

1½ teaspoons olive or jojoba oil

1½ teaspoons vitamin E oil

4 drops lemon essential oil

HOW YOU MAKE IT

Combine all the ingredients in a small jar or bottle and shake to mix thoroughly.

Sparkle Nail Soak

Lemon and baking soda have wonderful whitening properties that eliminate stains and brighten your nails. Follow this soak with the Moisturizing Hand Scrub (page 136).

WHAT YOU NEED

+ Juice of 1 lemon

+ 2 teaspoons baking soda

+ Bowl of warm water

+ Toothbrush

WHAT YOU DO

1. Add the lemon juice and baking soda to the bowl of warm water. Stir until the baking soda is dissolved.

2. Soak both your hands in the water for 10 minutes.

3. Scrub with a toothbrush around your nails and cuticles to thoroughly clean them. Be sure to scrub under your nails, too. Then rinse and dry your hands.

MOISTURIZING HAND SCRUB

MAKES ⅔ CUP

Hands can get so dry and chapped that creams sometimes have little chance of working their way past the tough outer layer to really moisturize deep down. Exfoliation removes dead skin cells to make hand creams more effective. Store this scrub in a small airtight container.

WHAT YOU NEED

1 tablespoon coconut oil

3 tablespoons sugar

2 tablespoons raw honey

2 tablespoons sea salt

1 tablespoon lemon juice

HOW YOU MAKE IT

1. If the coconut oil is solid, melt it in a microwave or a double boiler.

2. Combine the coconut oil with the remaining ingredients in a small bowl and stir until fully mixed.

HOW YOU USE IT

Once a week, as part of a manicure or as a stand-alone beauty treatment, massage this scrub all over your hands. Then rinse with warm water and pat dry.

moisturizing Hand scrub

EXTRA-RICH HAND CREAM

MAKES ½ CUP

Your hands get washed (hopefully!) more than any other part of your body, which can result in dry skin. The extra-deep moisture of this thick cream is especially helpful for dry hands. Massage it into your hands regularly.

HOW YOU MAKE IT

1. Combine the shea butter, almond oil, and beeswax in a double boiler. Warm over low heat, stirring gently, until the fats have melted and the ingredients are thoroughly combined.

2. Remove from the heat and stir in the essential oil.

3. Let the cream sit for at least 30 minutes to thicken, then transfer it to a jar or tin. Once the cream is completely cool, place the lid on the container.

WHAT YOU NEED

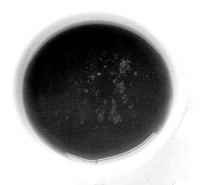

¼ cup shea butter

2 tablespoons almond oil or coconut oil

1 tablespoon beeswax

10 drops lavender essential oil

POLISH LIKE A PRO

Before you polish, dip a cotton swab in hand cream and trace it around each nail. This way, polish won't stick as easily to your skin, and you'll have a neat, professional-looking finish. And remember: practice makes perfect!

1. Place a drop of polish at the base of a nail but not all the way down to the cuticle.

2. Carefully brush the polish downward, almost to the cuticle, and then up to the tip of the nail.

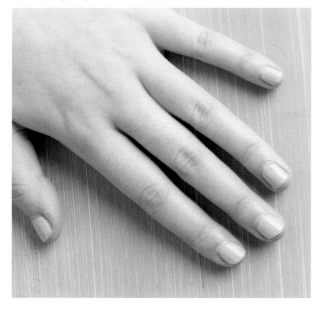

3. Apply a second stroke on each side, leaving a small gap between the skin and nail.

Tips and Tricks

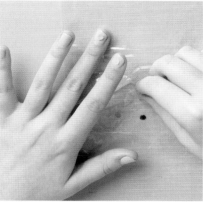

Paint nail polish shapes and designs on a plastic sandwich bag. Let the polish dry, and then peel the designs off the bag. Apply your designs to dry painted nails. Seal them in place with a clear topcoat. You can also paint designs and dot art directly on your nails with a toothpick.

Create geometric shapes on your nails with two contrasting polish colors and clear tape. Paint the first color on all of your nails. When it's dry, add strips of tape to your nails in stripes or diagonals. Paint the second color on the parts of your nails not covered in tape. Remove the tape and voilà!

Dry polished nails quickly using a bowl filled with water and ice cubes. Dip your newly painted fingernails in, and they'll dry in the blink of an eye!

WHAT'S THE DIFFERENCE?

If you choose to polish your toenails, follow the application steps above with one little twist: separate your toes to keep the polish tidy. This is essential! You can purchase foam toe dividers or simply scrunch up little bits of tissue and tuck them between your toes.

Polish, Naturally

Standard nail polish is one of the most toxic beauty products on the market today. The ingredients are bad for the environment and for YOU, since your nails absorb them.

Luckily, these days there are lots of natural polish options that are free of toluene, dibutyl phthalate (DBP), and formaldehyde, all harmful chemicals used in traditional polishes. These safer nail polishes are available in a wide selection of colors; look for them online and at stores that sell natural cosmetics. You can also make your own shades by adding some mica (readily available online) to a natural clear polish for a little DIY fun.

ZESTY FOOT SCRUB

MAKES ½ CUP

Show your tootsies some love by massaging them with a scoop of this minty citrus scrub. For a thorough foot-soothing treatment, slip them into the Fizzy Foot Soak (page 142) afterward.

WHAT YOU NEED

- ¼ cup coconut oil
- ¼ cup sugar
- 1 teaspoon finely grated lemon peel
- 5 drops lemon essential oil
- 5 drops peppermint essential oil

HOW YOU MAKE IT

1. If the coconut oil is solid, melt it in a microwave or a double boiler.

2. Combine all the ingredients in a glass jar and mix well.

HOW YOU USE IT

1. Sit near the bathtub or a dishpan filled with hot water, with your feet on a towel.

2. Massage about 1 tablespoon of the scrub over your entire foot and up the ankles. Repeat on the other foot.

3. Rinse your feet in the tub or in your warm footbath.

Fizzy Foot Soak

After a long day your tired feet will appreciate this invigorating bath. Vinegar and baking soda create a perfect reaction of bubbles, while tea tree oil destroys odors and bacteria. Try this refreshing treatment immediately following the Zesty Foot Scrub (page 141).

WHAT YOU NEED

+ Large towel
+ Dishpan or large bowl
+ Hot water
+ ½ cup Epsom salt
+ ¼ cup apple cider vinegar
+ ¼ cup bentonite clay
+ 5 drops tea tree essential oil
+ ¼ cup baking soda

WHAT YOU DO

1. Fold a large towel and place it in front of a comfy sitting spot, like a cozy chair or a corner of your sofa.

2. Fill a dishpan or large bowl with very hot water and set it on the towel.

3. Sprinkle the salt, vinegar, clay, and essential oil into the water and stir well. Then stir in the baking soda. Have a seat, slip your feet in, and relax.

HEALING HEEL STICK

MAKES 1 STICK

Dry, cracked heels don't stand a chance against this handy stick that puts moisture directly where it's needed without any mess. Rub it on your heels before going to bed each night, and you will wake up to smooth feet. Try it on your elbows and knees, too! For this recipe you'll need an empty deodorant tube, which you can buy new online or sterilize and reuse one you already have.

WHAT YOU NEED

3 tablespoons beeswax

3 tablespoons coconut oil

8 drops peppermint essential oil

HOW YOU MAKE IT

1. Combine the beeswax and coconut oil in a double boiler, and warm over low heat, stirring gently, until they are melted.

2. Remove from the heat and stir in the essential oil.

3. Carefully pour the mixture into a deodorant tube. Let it cool completely before putting on the lid.

SWEET FEET FOOT POWDER

MAKES ¾ CUP

Eliminate stinky feet by shaking this powder into your shoes at the end of the day. In the morning, tap out the powder before putting on your shoes. The powder will soak into your shoe overnight to kill bacteria, absorb odors, and keep you feeling fresh all day long.

WHAT YOU NEED

½ cup cornstarch or arrowroot powder

¼ cup baking soda

10 drops peppermint essential oil

10 drops tea tree essential oil

HOW YOU MAKE IT

Combine all the ingredients in a jar with a shaker lid. With the cover on, shake the jar to mix thoroughly.

Spa Slippers

These slippers are the ultimate in footwear for any self-care day or pedicure. Make a pair that fits you perfectly by tracing your feet, and wear them to keep your feet cozy while you paint your toenails!

WHAT YOU NEED

+ 2 sheets of paper
+ Pencil or pen
+ 18- by 18-inch piece of thick fleece or felted wool
+ Scissors or pinking shears
+ Straight pins
+ Sewing needle
+ Thread
+ Button (optional)
+ Puffy paint (available at most craft stores)

HOW YOU MAKE THEM

Create a pattern by tracing one of your feet on a piece of paper. Draw the straps on the sides of your feet as shown in step 2. Cut out your pattern.

Place your pattern on top of the fleece, pin it in place, then cut around the pattern using sharp scissors or pinking shears.

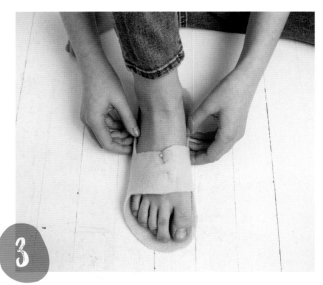

Place your bare foot on the sole of the pattern and fold both straps so that they overlap one another. The strap on the outside of the foot goes on top. Carefully pin the straps in place.

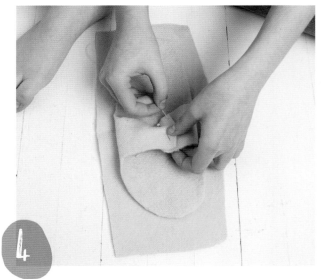

Stitch the straps in place with a needle and thread. Repeat steps 1–4 with your other foot to make a second slipper.

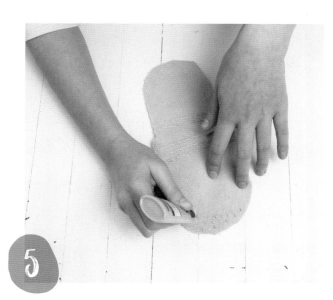

5

Dot the bottom sole of each slipper with puffy paint to give them some anti-skid properties. Let the paint dry thoroughly to the touch before walking in your slippers.

For extra pizzazz, sew a button on the strap!

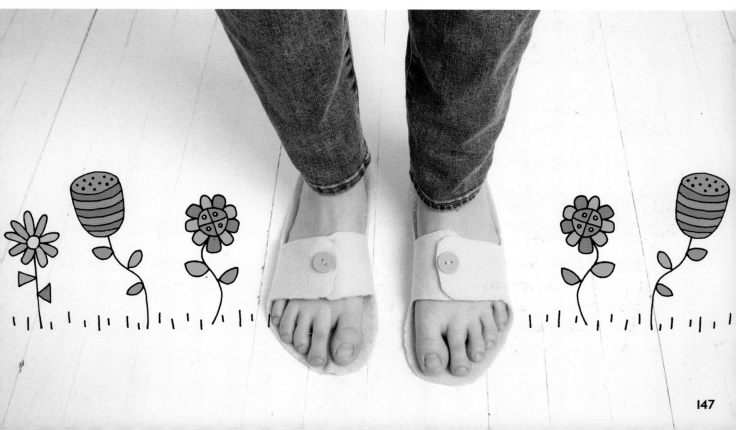

BEDTIME FOOT MASSAGE

Foot reflexology is a wonderful way to boost your health and help you feel great. This ancient practice is based on the theory that there is a connection between points on the soles of your feet and the organs and glands in your body. When you push on a specific point on your foot and feel discomfort or tenderness, it means that the corresponding body part needs extra attention.

You can practice reflexology all by yourself using the chart on the opposite page. Try making this a regular part of your nighttime routine to help you sleep deeply and wake up refreshed.

1. Prepare your feet with a simple wash in the tub with soap and warm water.

2. Moisturize your hands with coconut or almond oil so they can glide easily over your feet.

3. Starting with the big toe on one foot, squeeze, pull, and twist from the joint to the tip. Repeat on each toe of that foot.

4. Use your thumbs to massage the entire sole of your foot, from toes to heel. Apply firm pressure to each area on your foot for several seconds. Note any places that are particularly tender, and refer to the reflexology chart to identify the corresponding body part. It's fascinating to see which parts of your body might need more attention.

5. Massage the heel, Achilles tendon (above the heel), and ankle.

6. Finish off by massaging the whole top of the foot, from the ankle to the toes.

7. Repeat the entire process on the other foot.

FOOT REFLEXOLOGY

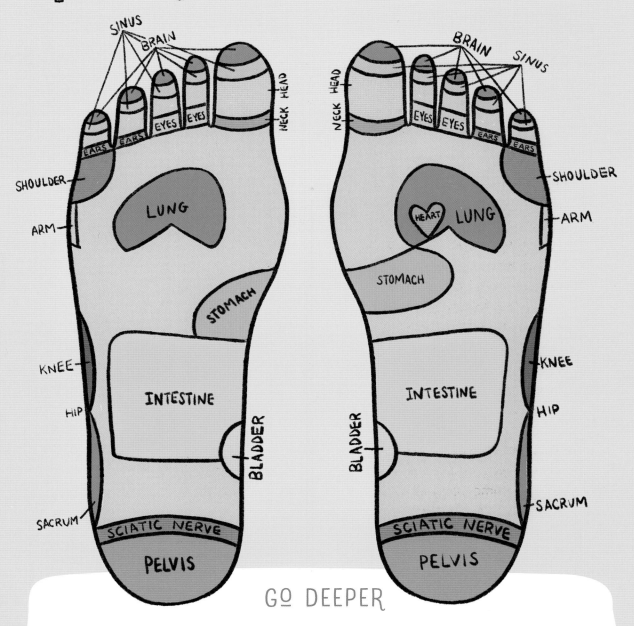

GO DEEPER

The benefits of foot reflexology are so great that you should fit in a little foot rub whenever you have a free moment, not just at bedtime. No matter when you do it, this kind of deep massage can release toxins into your bloodstream. To flush them out, drink a glass of water when you are finished with your massage.

Glossary:
Stocking Your Home Spa Lab

This glossary will set you up for success by familiarizing you with the ingredients and supplies you'll use the most.

In Your Toolbox

You can make most of the recipes in this book using basic cooking tools that probably are already in your kitchen. Nonporous materials like glass and stainless steel work best because they don't leach into the ingredients. For the most part, you can continue to cook with all of the equipment you use to create your spa recipes. Just make sure you wash each item well between uses. There is one exception: beeswax needs its own designated bowl or pot since it gets really sticky when melted and you'll never get all the wax residue off.

KITCHEN CLEANUP

Use hot water and baking soda to wash away any oily residue left on your kitchen tools.

Electric mixer with attachments

Glass or stainless steel mixing bowls

Double boiler

Mixing spoons

Funnel

1-cup glass measuring container with pouring spout (a second larger measuring cup is often helpful)

Assorted measuring cups

Whisk

Assorted measuring spoons

Double What?

A double boiler is a pair of pans, one of which fits inside the other. You put a couple of inches of water in the bottom pan, put the second pan on top, and set the pans over low heat. As the water in the bottom pan turns to steam, it gently heats whatever ingredients you put in the top pan without scorching or burning them. Using a double boiler is an effective way to melt oils and waxes that are solid at room temperature.

Melting ingredients with a double boiler can be a slow process. Keep an extra cup of water and oven mitts nearby in case you need to carefully add more water to the bottom pan if it runs low before your oil or wax is fully melted.

No double boiler? No worries! You can make your own. All you need is a pot and a stainless steel bowl that can fit into it securely without any gaps. The bottom of the bowl should not touch the bottom of the pot.

Storage and Containers

The recipes in this book make small batches of personal-care products. Your creations won't have any preservatives, so most should be used up within several weeks. Keep them in a cool, dry place, and use your best judgment if a product seems like it's past its prime. If you see any discolorations or if unpleasant scents take over, discard your product; these are signs that it has spoiled.

Finding cute containers for your products is one of the fun parts of making your own beauty blends. You can buy new containers in all shapes and sizes online, but you can also find spray bottles and other small containers in the travel section of most drugstores and supermarkets.

Recycling lip balm tins, deodorant tubes, or small jars and bottles is also an option. Just make sure you clean them out thoroughly before filling them with your homemade products. Some dishwashers have a sterilization cycle, and in that case, running your containers through the dishwasher is the easiest way to sterilize them. If you don't have a dishwasher, sterilize your containers in a pot of gently boiling water for 10 minutes to eliminate any bacteria.

No matter where you get your containers, I recommend glass and metal to store most of the products. Avoid storing your formulas in plastic containers if you can because plastic's chemicals easily seep into hot or high-fat products. If you must use plastic storage containers, use them for products that will be used up quickly, so that they sit in plastic for as little time as possible.

Label your containers so that you can identify what's inside them. Store all of your finished products and ingredients in a cool, dry, dark place unless refrigeration is specified in the recipe.

Get to Know Your Ingredients

You probably already have in your kitchen some of the ingredients you'll need to make the recipes in this book. But even if you don't, there's no need to run out and purchase tons of expensive stuff right away. Decide which recipes you'd like to make first, look around your kitchen to see what's already there, and make a grocery list of what else you'll need.

You'll use the following ingredients most often in these recipes. Here are a few reasons why they're good for you and some places where you can find them.

Aloe vera gel. People have used aloe since ancient times to heal wounds. You may have even slathered on aloe gel to help cool your skin after getting a sunburn. It also heals and dries out acne and infections. You can get aloe vera gel from a cutting from a houseplant or purchase it in a bottle. If you're buying the gel, get at least 99 percent pure aloe vera so that you avoid putting lots of additives and preservatives on your skin. You can buy pure aloe gel at many health food stores and online; the versions available in most supermarkets and pharmacies contain added chemicals.

Apple cider vinegar. This naturally fermented liquid helps to balance and maintain a healthy blood sugar level in your body. You can use apple cider vinegar topically on your skin for acne or drink it diluted in water for better digestion. Find it at the supermarket or health food store. Look for "raw" apple cider vinegar that contains the "mother," the beneficial bacteria that makes it more powerful and healing than any other vinegar.

Baking soda. Not just for baking! Baking soda relieves itchy skin and gently exfoliates and brightens skin. You can find it in the baking aisle of every supermarket.

Beeswax. This wax naturally hardens products like balms and deodorants, while also adding moisture. It's made by honeybees, which use it to make cells for storing honey in their hives. Some health food stores carry beeswax in blocks in the bulk section. You can also buy it online in blocks or in small pellets, which melt quickly and are easy to measure.

Bentonite clay. Created from finely ground rocks and ash, this thickening agent also draws out embedded dirt from pores and soothes bug bites and stings. Check the bulk section at your health food store or buy it online.

Cocoa butter. Smelling slightly like chocolate, this natural moisturizer melts at room temperature and blends well with other oils. You can easily find it online.

Coconut oil. At room temperature, this lightly fragrant oil is semisolid and white. Upon contact with the skin, it softens. This versatile ingredient is extracted from the meat of mature coconuts. It's a mighty moisturizer and helps strengthen the connective tissues in skin. Use an unrefined variety in body care recipes; find it in the oil aisle at the grocery store.

Epsom salt. Soaking in this magnesium-rich salt will improve your circulation and help relieve sore muscles. Epsom salt is readily available at drugstores and supermarkets.

Essential oils. Essential oils are extremely powerful liquids that are distilled from plant leaves, bark, flowers, seeds, fruit, and roots. You can find essential oils at your local health food store or buy them online.

Honey. In addition to being delicious to eat, this sticky, sweet substance is also a powerful skin moisturizer. To reap the full healing benefits, use raw (unpasteurized) honey, which is full of nutrients and enzymes; you can find it at farmers' markets, health food stores, and some supermarkets.

Jojoba oil. Pressed from the seed of a desert shrub, jojoba oil closely resembles sebum, the oil that your own skin produces. This makes it a great ingredient for face- and body-care products. Many health food stores carry jojoba oil, and you can easily find it online.

Oat flour. Grind up rolled oats to create this fine powder that moisturizes skin and absorbs oil at the same time. Buy rolled oats at the grocery store.

Sea salt. This common ingredient contains important nutrients that are good for your skin, while its abrasive texture makes a wonderful exfoliator. Sea salt is readily available at the supermarket.

Shea butter. This deeply nourishing moisturizer is a wonderful thickener in creams. Buy it at health food stores or online.

Turmeric. This yellow spice has anti-inflammatory properties, so it's wonderful for your insides! It's also well known for its skin-clearing and skin-brightening powers. You can find ground turmeric in the spice section of most grocery stores.

Witch hazel. This versatile refreshing liquid comes from the witch hazel bush, which has bright yellow flowers and grows in many front yards across North America. The liquid can be used for everything from taking the itch out of bug bites to spot-healing pimples. Health food stores, supermarkets, and drugstores all carry witch hazel.

The Essence of Essential Oils

Many essential oils offer health benefits for your whole body and can help make your personal-care products smell amazing. They play a significant role in many recipes, even though they call for only VERY small amounts. Measuring essential oils by the drop is easy since they often come in little glass bottles with drop-by-drop dispensers.

Because essential oils are such highly concentrated substances, you should never put them directly on your skin. Doing so can actually irritate or even harm your skin.

Always mix essential oils with distilled or purified water or some kind of *carrier oil,* which is simply a neutral, gentle vegetable or nut oil. Coconut oil and jojoba oil are wonderful carrier oils for skin care.

There are dozens of varieties of essential oils, and each one offers different health benefits depending on what plant it came from. To keep things simple for you, I've included just a few kinds of essential oils in the recipes in this book. Here are the ones you'll use the most.

Lavender: disinfectant and calming to the nervous system

Lemon: antibacterial, antifungal, and soothing but also uplifting

Peppermint: cooling and freshening, plus soothing to sore muscles

Tea tree: antibacterial and antifungal

Metric Conversion Chart

To convert	to	multiply
teaspoons	milliliters	teaspoons by 4.93
tablespoons	milliliters	tablespoons by 14.79
cups	milliliters	cups by 236.59
cups	liters	cups by 0.24
inches	centimeters	inches by 2.54
pounds	grams	pounds by 453.59

Acknowledgments

I'm deeply grateful for all of the wonderful energy and collaboration that went into creating this book. Big thanks to:

My daughter, Noemi, and all of her good friends for testing and perfecting our recipes.

My aunt Amy, who gave me my first natural body-care book and instilled a lifelong love for concocting potions and lotions.

Winky, and her crew of girls, who brought this book to life in her beautiful home studio.

Catrine, whose discerning eye allowed me to relax and trust that natural beauty would shine through on the pages.

Michal, for her sweet support, respect, and careful editorial eye.

Linda, who keeps me smiling and always has my back.

INDEX

Keep the Fun Flowing
with More Storey Books

by Deanna F. Cook

This fresh, fun cookbook teaches basic cooking techniques in kid-friendly language, with dozens of recipes (and stickers!) for favorite foods like French toast, homemade granola, Buffalo chicken fingers, tortilla chips, and much more.

by Emily K. Neuburger

Make a visual day-in-your-life map, turn random splotches into quirky characters for a playful story, and list the things that make you you! These 60 interactive writing prompts and art how-tos will help spur your imaginative self-expression.

by Jonathan Adolph

From water fireworks and soda stalactites to a caterpillar hatchery, a balloon barometer, and much more, you can conduct these 40 fun, foolproof, and fascinating science experiments in a glass canning jar.

by Nicole Blum & Catherine Newman

Create, hack, or customize! Step-by-step directions show you the basics of how to sew, embroider, knit, crochet, weave, and felt. You can then use your new skills to hand-make cool bracelets, backpacks, merit badges, keychains, and more.